DIVIDED AMERICA

An AP Guide to the Fracturing of a Nation

The Associated Press

Edited by Jerry Schwartz

D1431219

The Associated Press
450 West 33rd Street
New York, NY 10001
www.ap.org

Edited by Jerry Schwartz
Project Management by Peter Costanzo
Design and Production by BNGO Books
Cover Design by Tommy Browne

Visit AP Books: www.ap.org/books

All photographs provided by AP Images: www.apimages.com

Contents

Appendix

A Message from the AP Newsroom
Kathleen Carroll, Executive Editor, The Associated Press

Early in 2016, it was clear that a lot of strong feelings were bubbling up in places across the United States. And while AP has journalists in every state covering every possible topic, we needed a different approach to under- stand what Americans were feeling and why. There was no more important story in the country than that. So we pulled together a rich cross-section of AP journalists from different backgrounds and locations and sent them out to talk with people. To hear what was on their minds.

It was fascinating and sobering. We found people deeply invested in a number of very important topics: jobs, immigration, morality, civil- ity, drugs, race and lots of worries large and small. We found optimism and hope and joy. We found frustration and anger, disappointment and despair. And on any given topic, we found people to be deeply divided and having a hard time talking with folks on the other side.

We kept talking to Americans and they gave us the stories that you will find here. Each one is a rich examination of the topics most important to people throughout the nation. Together, the stories form a compelling portrait of a nation and its people at a complex and important time in the nation's history.

"It is not our differences that divide us.
It is our inability to recognize, accept, and celebrate those differences."
— The poet Audre Lorde

Pondering whether America's still great

Americans agree on this much: They are disgusted with politics.

They look toward Washington and see a broken federal government, a place where politicians seem more interested in self-preservation than We the People. Things don't seem much better in state capitals, and, who knows? Lead-tainted water may be pouring out of their kitchen faucet next. Yet Americans say they still believe in America, the experiment in democracy that the founders described as a place where the government should protect the rights of ordinary people to life, liberty and the pursuit of happiness. There's something at the core of America they long for, even if it's hard to define and seems distant in 2016.

Donald Trump proclaims he will "make America great again." Hillary Clinton counters that America "has never stopped being great." But what does that even mean? And who defines greatness? A billionaire businessman, a former secretary of state—or an aging musician in New Orleans? What about the woman in Illinois who served in the U.S. military in Afghanistan? Or the industrial worker worried about his job in Alabama?

The Associated Press interviewed a wide range of Americans to get a sense of what they think about the nation's greatness in the twilight of President Barack Obama's eight years in office. The responses were as different as Americans themselves, yet a theme emerged: Compared to other nations, the United States is at least good, probably even great. But there's a lot of work to be done. "Yes, America is great. It could be a lot better if the politicians weren't fighting each other all the time . . . ," said Rodney Kimball, a 74-year-old stove dealer in West Bethel, Maine. "The government needs to start doing what's right for the people."

America is divided by political party, choice of media, income, gender, race or ethnic group, religious faith (or not), generation, geography and general outlook on the country's future. Pundits have proclaimed the electorate angry and wondered if the nation can ever recover the sense of unity experienced in the immediate aftermath of the al-Qaida attacks that took place 15 years ago this September.

The current dearth of confidence in the nation's politics and government is striking. Recent polling by the AP and the NORC Center for Public Affairs Research shows just 13 percent of Americans are proud of the 2016 election, and 55 percent feel helpless. Only 10 percent have a great deal of confidence in the overall political system, with 4 percent having a great deal of confidence in Congress, 15 percent in the executive branch, and 24 percent in the Supreme Court. Few Americans see either political party as responsive to ordinary voters.

Although their America is still a land of shining seas, spacious skies and majestic mountains, many express a deep sense of disenchantment and uncertainty in their own lives. "I think that America as an idea is one of the most beautiful ideas that the world has ever known. I think that American opportunity and ingenuity has built some of the most incredible technologies and innovations today," said Allene Swanson, 22, of Chicago. "And still, when I look around, I see a country that seems like it's crumbling. I see people who are hungry and broke and who are struggling a lot."

For some, real success has always seemed out of reach. The old textile mill across town is a reminder, dark and empty because labor was cheaper in Southeast Asia or Latin America; the manufacturing plant on the outskirts of the city uses steel imported from China. Employment has rebounded since the Great Recession, but wages are stagnant. Forget saving for a home—millions work more than one job just to keep food on the table and the lights on. What happened to the American dream? That's what is being asked in places like inner city St. Louis, home to 32-year-old Craig House. He lives with his grandmother in a sea of burned-out buildings and abandoned schools not far from a hip, trendy part of town. "America has always been great, just not for me and my people. For us it's been the worst ever," said House, shaking his head as he takes a long drag off his cigarette. "People come from all over the world, Arabs own this, that. Black man don't own nothing."

Known as "Deacon" in his native New Orleans, 74-year-old guitarist John Moore remembers a time when America was headed in the right direction, when everything seemed to be coming together. It was in the 1960s, when black people like Moore were seeing an end to racial segregation; when women were gaining equality; when politicians were taking a stand to end poverty despite the turmoil of protests over the Vietnam War. "Those were the best years," said Moore, tears welling in his eyes in the living room-turned-recording studio of his shotgun house. "And then they were destroyed right before my very eyes when they assassinated all of our leaders. Robert Kennedy. John Kennedy. Martin Luther King. Malcolm X. All of our leaders. And, you know, that was the end of hope. We had no more hope."

Hope returned, at least for some, in 2008 when a mixed-race lawyer with a foreign-sounding name won the White House. Obama's election seemed to prove that anyone could accomplish anything in America. Yet the years that followed have seemed more unsettling than uplifting to many. Today, some people want more from their government. Others just want it to go away as much as possible. "I expect less government, less regulation," said Russ Madson, 45, a steel industry worker looking for better opportunities in Birmingham, Alabama. "Our country was built by people like the Rockefellers, Edison, Henry Ford—pioneers. And today they couldn't do what they did because of regulation."

But others expect more of government. Agriculture consultant and farmer Mike Poling of Delphos, Ohio, expects good governance and leadership "and nothing less." "That's what got us to this point and that's what made America great," said Poling, 58. "What made America great is its people. That's what built the country. Our forefathers had the foresight to draft the Constitution, the Bill of Rights that has laid the groundwork for (the) nation carrying on for 200 years and continues to guide us."

Yet American greatness isn't just about words scrawled on yellowed paper and kept in a vault at the National Archives. A veteran of the war in Afghanistan, daughter of immigrants from Hong Kong, 29-year-old Kimberly Jung sees it as something deeper, a challenge to every citizen.

"I believe greatness is a responsibility," said Jung, of Chicago. "It's a dual state of mind in which you know your power or you know what resources you have but also your weaknesses. And you harness that set of strengths and weaknesses to work with a group and form a team and do great things."

That striving for the common good is somehow AWOL in America right now, people say. "If there was one thing I could change about this country it would be to sit here and get us focused back on the country itself and not on our own self-interest," said Poling, the Ohio farmer. "I think we've lost track of what built this country, and that is the fact we came together as a body of one to build it and make it great."

In a sprawling country of 319 million people, it's easy for most anyone to tuck themselves away in suburbia, the rural heartland, an urban ghetto or a gentrified neighborhood and see only those things outside the front window or just down the street. People can turn on the echo chamber of cable TV or the internet and forget what high school student Dana Craig says America really is: A great place built on the idea that everyone should get an equal opportunity, a chance. "Throughout history (I am) not sure we did the best job in keeping up with these principles and reaching those goals in the way that we want to, but I think what defines our greatness is our ability to continue working toward these goals even if we are not necessarily perfect in them," said Craig, 15, of River Falls, Wisconsin.

Whether they opt for Trump, Clinton or someone else this November, Americans say the state of the union isn't good enough. Amal Kassir sees her own future caught up with the chance the country has right now to make itself into something better. Kassir, a 20-year-old college student in Colorado, was born in Denver to a father from Syria and a mother from America. A poet who also works in her family's Middle Eastern restaurant, Kassir describes her own life as being intertwined with that of the United States. Is America great? Yes, she says. And it's also her best chance. "No doubt whatever greatness I'm capable of comes from being in this place," she said.

—Jay Reeves and Robin McDowell, AP Correspondents

Benton, Kentucky
Evangelicals feel alienated, anxious

Picture a country church on a Sunday morning: congregants greeting each other with hugs and handshakes, the choir warming up for the day's service. Then imagine journalists from one of the biggest news organizations in the world descending, preparing to report on what members of the church were thinking about some critical, and sensitive, issues.

This was the scene when a photographer, videographer and I descended on Christian Fellowship church. The pastor, Richie Clendenen, warmly welcomed us, even though some in the congregation were deeply worried about what we would report and how they would be depicted. Our goal was to help explain why evangelicals were feeling vulnerable, despite their large numbers and influence.

The story drew a mixed reaction: gratitude from many conservative Christians that a news organization had taken the time to explain why they were so apprehensive, and criticism from some liberals and others upset that evangelicals envisioned themselves in any way as victims. We felt it was an important story to tell since this unease will play a major role in how evangelicals vote and shape public policy in the years ahead.

— Rachel Zoll, AP National Religion Writer

* * *

Pastor Richie Clendenen stepped away from the pulpit, microphone in hand. He walked the aisles of the Christian Fellowship Church, his voice rising to describe the perils believers face in 21st-century America.

"The Bible says in this life you will have troubles, you will have persecutions. And Jesus takes it a step further: You'll be hated by all nations for my name's sake," he said.

"Let me tell you," the minister said, "that time is here."

The faithful in the pews needed little convincing. Even in this deeply religious swath of western Kentucky—a state where about half the residents are evangelical—conservative Christians feel under siege.

For decades, they say, they have been steadily pushed to the sidelines of American life and have come under attack for their most deeply held beliefs, born of their reading of Scripture and their religious mandate to evangelize. The 1960s ban on prayer in public schools is still a fresh wound. Every legal challenge to a public Nativity scene or Ten Commandments display is another marginalization. They've been "steamrolled," they say, and "misunderstood."

Religious conservatives could once count on their neighbors to at least share their view of marriage. Those days are gone. Public opinion on same-sex relationships turned against conservatives even before the U.S. Supreme Court legalized gay marriage nationwide.

Now, many evangelicals say liberals want to seal their cultural victory by silencing the church. Liberals call this paranoid. But evangelicals see evidence of the threat in every new uproar over someone asserting a right to refuse recognition of same-sex marriages—whether it be a baker, a government clerk, or the leaders of religious charities and schools.

America's divisions—right-left, urban-rural, black-white and more—spill daily into people's lives, from their relations with each other, to their harsh communications on social media, to their decisions in an acrimonious presidential election campaign. Many Christian conservatives feel there is another, less recognized chasm in American life, and they find themselves on the other side of the divide between "us" and "them."

Clendenen, preaching on this recent Sunday, reflected on the chasm between his congregants and other Americans.

"There's nobody hated more in this nation than Christians," he said, amid nods and cries of encouragement. "Welcome to America's most wanted: You."

Lead pastor Richie Clendenen speaks during a service at the Christian Fellowship Church in Benton, KY, April 10, 2016. (AP Photo/David Goldman)

For evangelicals like those at Christian Fellowship, the sense of a painful reckoning is not just imagined; their declining clout in public life can be measured.

The turnabout is astonishing and hard to grasp—for them and for other Americans—since the U.S. remains solidly religious and Christian, and evangelicals are still a formidable bloc in the Republican Party. But a series of losses in church membership and in public policy battles, along with America's changing demographics, are weakening evangelical influence, even in some of the most conservative regions of the country.

"The shift in the last few years has really been stunning," said Ed Stetzer, executive director of Lifeway Research, an evangelical consulting firm in Nashville, Tennessee. "Nobody would have guessed the pace of change. That's why so many people are yelling we have to take our country back."

The Protestant majority that dominated American culture through the nation's history is now a Protestant minority. Their share of the population dipped below 50 percent sometime after 2008.

Liberal-leaning Protestant groups, such as Presbyterians and Lutherans, started shrinking earlier, but some evangelical churches are now in decline. The conservative Southern Baptist Convention lost 200,000 from its ranks in 2014 alone, dropping to 15.5 million, its smallest number in more than two decades.

The trend is reflected in the highest reaches of public life. The U.S. Supreme Court is now comprised completely of Jews and Roman Catholics. In the 2012 presidential election, the Republican nominees were a Mormon, Mitt Romney, and a Catholic, Paul Ryan.

"We've lost our home field advantage," Stetzer said.

At the same time, the Bible Belt, as a cultural force, is collapsing, said the Rev. Russell Moore, head of the Southern Baptist public policy agency.

Nearly a quarter of Americans say they no longer affiliate with a faith tradition. It's the highest share ever recorded in surveys, indicating the stigma for not being religious has eased—even in heavily evangelical areas. Americans who say they have no ties to organized religion, dubbed "nones," now make up about 23 percent of the population, just behind evangelicals, who comprise about 25 percent, according to the Pew Research Center.

Christians who have been only nominally tied to a conservative church are steadily dropping out altogether. When Moore was growing up in Mississippi, any parent whose children weren't baptized by age 12 or 13 would face widespread disapproval, he said. Those times have passed.

"People don't have to be culturally identified with evangelical Christianity in order to be seen as good people, good neighbors or good Americans," Moore said.

Politically, old guard religious right organizations such as the Moral Majority and the Christian Coalition are greatly diminished or gone, and no broadly unifying leader or organization has replaced them. In this year's presidential race, the social policy issues championed by Christian conservatives are not central, even amid the furor over bathroom access for transgender people.

Clendenen said many in his church backed Texas Sen. Ted Cruz, who had positioned himself in the Republican primaries as the standard bearer for religious conservatives. Chris Haynes, a church band member and communications professor, said he voted for Ohio Gov. John Kasich. Some congregants now support presumptive nominee Donald Trump—a thrice-married, profane casino magnate with a record of positions at odds with social conservatism. "It's like we're scraping the bottom of the barrel," for candidates, said Haynes' wife, Brandi, who teaches at the Christian Fellowship school.

White evangelical voters remain very influential in early primaries. About two-thirds of Iowa caucus voters this year said they were born-again Christians. In Mississippi, eight in 10 primary voters were evangelical. And they turn out at high rates in general elections.

But white evangelicals can't match the growth rate of groups that tend to support Democrats—Latinos, younger people and Americans with no religious affiliation. In 2004, overwhelming evangelical support helped secure a second term for President George W. Bush, a Christian conservative who made social issues a priority. In 2012, evangelicals voted for Romney at the same rate—yet he lost.

This is a far cry from 1976, which Newsweek declared the "Year of the Evangelical," when born-again candidate Jimmy Carter won the presidency and more conservative Christians were drawn into politics. Four years later, Ronald Reagan famously recognized the emerging influence of the religious right, telling evangelicals in Dallas, "I know you can't endorse me, but I endorse you and what you're doing."

No issue has more starkly illuminated conservative Christians' waning influence than the struggle over same-sex marriage.

Evangelicals were "all in" with their opposition to gay rights starting back with the Moral Majority in the 1980s, said Robert Jones, author of "The End of White Christian America." In the 2004 election, Americans appeared to be on the same page, approving bans on same-sex marriage in all 11 states where the measures were on the ballot. When President

Barack Obama was first elected in 2008, just four in 10 Americans supported gay marriage.

But three years later, support rose to more than five in 10. And now the business wing of the Republican Party is deserting social conservatives on the issue, largely backing anti-discrimination policies for gays and transgender people. Younger Americans, including younger evangelicals, are especially accepting of same-sex relationships, which means evangelicals "have lost a generation on this issue," Jones said.

"This issue is so prominent and so symbolic," said Jones, chief executive of Public Religion Research Institute, which specializes in surveys about religion and public life. "It was such a decisive loss, not only in the actual courts, the legal courts, but also in the court of public opinion. They lost legally and they lost culturally."

Clendenen said he saw "a lot of fear, a lot of anger" in his church after the Supreme Court ruling. He said it made him feel that Christians like him had been pushed to the edge of a cliff.

"It has become the keystone issue," he said, sitting in his office, where photos of his father and grandfather, both preachers, are on display. "I

Leaflets sit in the window of the local Republican party office in Benton, KY. (AP Photo/David Goldman)

never thought we'd be in the place we are today. I never thought that the values I've held my whole life would bring us to a point where we were alienated or suppressed."

Trump uses rhetoric that has resonance for Christian conservatives who fear their teachings on marriage will soon be outlawed as hate speech.

"We're going to protect Christianity and I can say that," Trump has said. "I don't have to be politically correct."

If culture wars and the outside world once felt remote amid the soybean and tobacco farms around Marshall County, Kentucky, change of many kinds is now obvious to Clendenen's congregants.

Latino immigrants are starting to arrive in significant numbers, drawn partly by farm work. Muslims are working at chicken processing plants in the next county or enrolling at nearby Murray State University. On a recent weeknight, a group of women wearing abayas shopped in a Dollar General store near campus. Some gays and lesbians are out in the community, and Clendenen says he occasionally sees them at Sunday worship.

It was on the other side of Kentucky, in Rowan County, where clerk Kim Davis spent five days in jail last year for refusing on religious grounds to issue marriage licenses to same-sex couples since the licenses would include her name. Gov. Matt Bevin recently tried to defuse the conflict by signing a bill creating a form without a clerk's name.

In New Mexico and Oregon, a photographer and a baker were fined under nondiscrimination laws after refusing work for same-sex cere- monies. Daniel Slayden, a Christian Fellowship member and owner of Parcell's, a popular bakery and deli near the church, has never been asked to bake a wedding cake for a same-sex couple but already knows how he'd respond.

"If a homosexual couple comes in and wants a cake, then that's fine. I mean I'll do it as long as I'm free to speak my truth to them," said Slayden, taking a break after the lunchtime rush. "I don't want to get (to) any point to where I have to say or accept that their belief is the truth."

The problem, many religious conservatives say, is that government is growing more coercive in many areas bearing on their beliefs.

They say some colleges—citing a 2010 Supreme Court ruling that required school groups to accept all comers—are revoking recognition for Christian student clubs because they require their leaders to hold certain beliefs.

Some faith-based nonprofits with government contracts, such as Catholic Charities in Illinois, have shuttered adoption programs because of new state rules that say agencies with taxpayer funding can't refuse placements with same-sex couples.

And religious leaders worry that Christian schools and colleges will lose accreditation or tax-exempt status over their codes of conduct barring same-sex relationships.

A 1983 U.S. Supreme Court ruling allowed the IRS to revoke nonprofit status from religious schools that banned interracial dating. In the Supreme Court gay marriage case, U.S. Solicitor General Donald Verrilli, representing the government, was asked whether something similar could happen to Christian schools, which often provide housing for married students. He responded, "It's certainly going to be an issue," causing a meltdown across the evangelical blogosphere.

It has come to this: Many conservative Christians just don't feel welcome in their own country.

They say they are either mocked or erased in popular culture. "When was the last time you saw an evangelical or conservative Christian character portrayed positively on TV?" Stetzer asked.

"The idea of what we call biblical morality in our culture at large is completely laughed at and spurned as nonsense," said David Parish, a former pastor at Christian Fellowship and the son of its founder. "The church as an institution, as a public entity—we are moving more and more in conflict with the culture and with other agendas."

How to navigate this new reality? Most conservative Christians fall into one of three broad camps.

There are those who are determined to even more fiercely wage the culture wars, demanding the broadest possible religious exemptions from recognizing same-sex marriage.

There are those who plan to withdraw as much as possible into their own communities to preserve their faith—an approach dubbed the "Benedict Option," for a fifth-century saint who, disgusted by the decadence of Rome, fled to the forest where he lived as a hermit and prayed.

There is, however, a segment that advocates living as a "prophetic minority," confidently upholding their beliefs but in a gentler way that rejects the aggressive tone of the old religious right and takes up other issues, such as ending human trafficking, that can cross ideological lines.

Clendenen is cut from this mold. Now 38, he came of age when the religious right was at its apex, and he concluded any mix of partisan politics with Christianity was toxic for the church.

A congregant once lobbied him to participate in Pulpit Freedom Sunday, an annual conservative effort to defy IRS rules against backing politicians from the pulpit. Clendenen stood before the congregation and endorsed . . . Jesus.

He prays for President Barack Obama, considering it a Christian duty no matter his opposition to the president's policies. But Clendenen believes few Americans who support same-sex marriage would show him or his fellow evangelicals a similar level of respect. "On any front that we speak on, we're given this label of intolerance, we're given this label of hate," Clendenen said. (He said evangelicals are partly responsible for the backlash, however, because of the hateful language some used in the marriage debates. "I don't see the LGBT community as my enemy," he said.)

He uses the word persecution to describe what Christians are facing in the U.S., even though he feels strange doing so. He has traveled extensively to help start churches in other countries, and knows the violence many Christians endure. A map of the world is posted in his office with pins in the places he's visited, including Romania and Kenya. And yet, he feels the word applies here, too.

He ruminated on all of this as he prepared to head into his sanctuary to lead the Sunday service.

Some good may come of these hard times, he believes. Conservative Christians who have been complacent will have to decide just how much their religion matters "when there's a price to pay for it," he said. Christianity has often thrived in countries where it faces intense opposition, he noted.

Preaching now, Clendenen urged congregants to hold fast to their positions in a country that has grown hostile to them. And as the worship service wound down, he issued a final exhortation.

"Don't give up," he said. "Don't let your light go out."

Missoula, Montana
Neighbors at odds over refugees

It seemed an unlikely spot for a fierce debate to emerge over the issue of Syrian refugees.

The western corner of Montana is more than 6,500 miles from the war-torn nation and one of the most homogenous parts of America. But it was in that Big Sky country where I found tension, anger and a fear that appeared to be at odds with a place better known for its scenic mountains and laid-back college town atmosphere.

A plan to welcome a few dozen refugee families to the Missoula area had aroused these intense emotions. Muslim academics who'd lived in the area for decades *confided they felt a new sense of anxiety. And some long-time residents said they, too, were scared, worried that international terrorism could somehow land on their doorstep.*

To me, this conflict reflected the larger divide that was so much a part of this turbulent election year.

—Sharon Cohen, AP National Writer

* * *

For the world, the photograph of a Syrian 3-year-old in a red T-shirt and black sneakers, his lifeless body washed up on a Turkish beach, was a horrific symbol of the desperation of hundreds of thousands of refugees. For Mary Poole, a young mother haunted by "those little shoes . . . the little face," it was an inspiration.

She and members of her book club asked: Why not bring a small number of Syrian families to Missoula? She knows now that this was a "romantic" notion. "It wasn't even a grain of sand in my brain that people wouldn't want to help starving, drowning families. I didn't do this to be controversial. I didn't do this to stir the pot."

But it did. And what started as a disagreement over whether to welcome dozens of refugees to this peaceful corner of western Montana soon erupted into something much larger, encompassing wildly divergent views of Islam, big government and whether Americans should "take care of our own" before worrying about newcomers.

Neighboring counties—and in some cases, neighbors—locked horns.

Demonstrators took to the streets: "No Jobs, No Housing, No Free Anything," proclaimed some opponents' signs. Some warned that Islamic State terrorists could infiltrate their communities; others suggested that the federal government, long accused of tyranny in its dealings with the West, was at it again.

The refugees' supporters did not back off. "Rise Above Fear, Refugees Welcome" they declared.

Missoula's mayor, John Engen, was among them. "I think that the war on terror has produced an internal war on compassion," he says. "We have

Missoula Mayor John Engen exits city hall, April 14, 2016. (AP Photo/ Brennan Linsley)

been programmed to be very afraid since 9/11 and to think of people who aren't white Anglo-Saxon Americans as 'other' and we should be afraid of people who are 'other.'"

This did not occur in a vacuum. What's happened here reflects what's happening across the nation in an election year dominated by inflammatory rhetoric over immigration, including calls for building a border wall, the mass deportation of immigrants living in the country illegally, and temporarily banning Muslims from entering the U.S.

And more generally, Montanans are like other Americans who ask: How are we to live together, as one nation, when we are so estranged?

At a time when the public is polarized over issues ranging from gay marriage to guns, the Rev. Joseph Carver, pastor at St. Francis Xavier Parish, sees this as just another "incarnation of the larger divide in the country." His congregation, which gathers in a towering 124-year-old brick structure with frescoes, ornate scroll work, is overwhelmingly in favor of refugees.

Carver, like others here, believes the spark that ignited this conflict is fear. "Refugees," he declares, "are seen as a threat to our way of life."

Montana is a place of great beauty, with its snow-capped mountains, Ponderosa pines, bighorn sheep, bison and elk. Fly fishermen reel in trout from shimmering streams. College kids can be spotted kayaking on the Clark Fork River on cool spring nights. And a bookstore owner can point to the park down the street where a moose is known to frequent.

It is not, however, a diverse place. Though the sparsely populated state is home to seven Indian reservations, nearly nine of 10 residents are white, according to Census figures. Only about 2 percent are foreign-born. Since 2012, the state has welcomed just 13 refugees from Cuba and Iraq, according to officials.

But Missoula, site of a World War II detention center for Japanese-Americans, Italian merchant seamen and others, has a recent history of embracing refugees. The International Rescue Committee resettled the Hmong in the late 1970s and through the 1980s; some remain as farmers. Later, another agency brought Ukrainians and Belarusians here.

With its coffee houses, murals and bike trails, Missoula has a laid-back feel. It is home to the University of Montana, as well as a peace center named for Jeannette Rankin, a pacifist who was the first woman member of Congress—and the only vote against declaring war on Japan after the Pearl Harbor attack. The center's philosophy is captured on a wall lined with bumper stickers—"Peace is Patriotic," "Books Not Bombs" and "Practice Nonviolence"—and a stenciled message on a front window: "Refugees Welcome."

When Poole, a jewelry maker, and others formed a group called Soft Landing, they quickly expanded their plan to include not just Syrians but all refugees and turned to the International Rescue Committee to lead the resettlement. Their efforts were endorsed by the mayor, most council members and the three Democratic county commissioners, who sent letters to federal officials.

But Missoula is an island of progressive blue surrounded by a sea of conservative red, and often diverges politically from other communities in Montana.

Just to the south, in rural and Republican Ravalli County, a county commissioners' hearing over the issue was moved to a middle school gym to accommodate the hundreds who showed up for what turned into a raucous meeting. Several pro-refugee speakers were jeered. The commissioners formalized their opposition in their own letter to federal officials—and Flathead County, nearly 130 miles north of Missoula, did the same weeks later.

In testimony and letters in Ravalli County, those saying "no" outlined their objections. They argued that Muslims or others from the Middle East could create the kind of chaos seen in Europe, impose an enormous tax burden and wouldn't be able to assimilate because they don't share American values. Many said their biggest fear was the U.S. government couldn't conduct adequate screening. Some spoke of apocalyptic visions of terrorists posing as refugees making their way to the quiet countryside.

"There's no 800 number you can call into Morocco or Libya or any one of those places . . . and say, 'Can you check the identity of this person?' Without the ability to properly vet them, it's literally putting Americans' lives at risk," says Eli Anselmi, who felt compelled to write a letter even though he lives three hours away in Bozeman.

The risk may be minimal, he says, but the potential harm is great. "Let's say that you have a bowl of M&Ms . . . and there are two that have cyanide. Will you eat from that bowl?"

Ray Hawk, a Ravalli County commissioner, has similar worries. "These are folks that have declared war on the United States," he says. "Their war

Bookstore owner Shawn Wathen sees the rejection of refugees as a blend of misinformation, economic anxiety and fear of the unknown. (AP Photo/ Brennan Linsley)

is terrorism and that's the way they're going to do it. And I don't feel that we need to give them that chance. Now, if the government gets a handle on this thing and has a way to vet these people, I'm all for them. I love to see anybody come into America and succeed."

Supporters of the refugees weighed in with reminders of America's tradition of providing sanctuary to those who've fled war and oppression; some cited their own family history. They spoke of empathy, pointed to a lengthy screening process and noted the other refugees who resettled here successfully in recent decades.

Shawn Wathen, a bookstore owner in Ravalli County, was appalled his 18-year-old son was booed when he testified in support of the refugees and then later cursed by some opponents. Wathen wrote the commissioners, accusing them of "xenophobic grandstanding." One replied that he was "ignorant."

Wathen, who has called the sprawling Bitterroot Valley home for 20 years, sees the rejection of refugees as a blend of misinformation, economic anxiety and fear of the unknown.

"It surpasses any notion of reason . . . that kind of idea that they are not us, and therefore they pose a threat," he says. "There's just that sense the horde is out there and if we don't circle the wagons . . . we're going to be overrun and poor white America is going to suffer."

America has a long history of wariness of refugees.

Last November, shortly after the Paris terrorist attacks, a Gallup poll found that Americans, by 60 to 37 percent, opposed taking in refugees fleeing the Syrian civil war. In 1978, there was a 57 to 32 percent opposition to accepting Indochinese boat people, and in 1946, after World War II, the public was against welcoming displaced people from Europe, including Jews, by 72 to 16 percent.

Generally, Americans tend to favor refugees with whom they share some connection — political, religious or personal — and the public has little interaction with Muslims, says David Haines, a professor emeritus at George Mason University who has written extensively about refugees.

He says the public doesn't understand the rigorous vetting process. "The risks from refugees are really low because it's an extremely well-screened population," he says. "But it's hard for people to settle down on this issue, especially in a highly politicized context."

In Missoula, academics and religious leaders have expressed alarm about the harsh tone of the presidential campaign, especially comments aimed at Muslims by Donald Trump. In April, they sponsored "Celebrate Islam Week" at the university in hopes of countering the trend.

Among the participants was Samir Bitar, an Arabic studies professor who arrived at the University of Montana in the 1970s as a 16-year-old freshman, raised a family and has spent most of his adult life here.

Bitar has lectured for decades across the state without controversy— until this year, when about a dozen people in the nearby town of Darby objected to his planned talk at the library. The reason: They didn't want a Muslim in their town, according to the librarian. The library board voted. Bitar spoke and received a warm reception.

But the tone and atmosphere are decidedly different now, he says.

"This is the first time I actually look behind me as I walk. I've been here 42 years," he says. "It's like every part of my identity is coming under attack, including my American identity."

Recently, two students accepted Bitar's challenge to walk around wearing Muslim head gear to see how people would react. One young man donned a kufi, or skull cap, and classmates wouldn't sit next to him, Bitar says. While working at a deli, the student was rebuffed by a customer's wife who said: "'We're not going to have a Muslim help us.'"

Bitar, who is Palestinian, finds it all disheartening. People now are "motivated by pure emotion and not really thinking in logical terms," he says. "Fear turns into hatred."

Jameel Chaudhry, the campus architect, a native of Kenya and another member of the small Muslim community, says he, too, senses a new hostility.

"All of a sudden WE are the problem," he says. "We've never had this before, and I've been here 20 years. We didn't have this even after 9/11."

Chaudhry attributes this attitude to Trump, accusing the presumptive Republican nominee of stoking fears for political gain.

"He's become the champion of the anti-Muslim, anti-refugee movement," he says. While that group talks of being tired of political correctness, Chaudhry sees something else: "They don't want the other races coming in here."

Jameel Chaudhry, a native of Kenya and a member of a small Muslim community, says he senses a new hostility. (AP Photo/Brennan Linsley)

But those who've publicly spoken out against refugees bristle at suggestions they're racist. They say they'retrying to protect their communities.

"It doesn't make any difference if they're Muslims, Russians, whatever. You have to know who they are, what they've been doing in the past," says Jim Buterbaugh, a construction worker who organized three opposition rallies, including one at the state Capitol. "Are you going to go downtown and take five people off the streets and move them into your house without knowing who they are? Nobody in their right mind would do that."

He and others are upset they have no vote on this issue. State and local governments legally don't have authority to bar refugees, though they can refuse to directly provide local services, according to Haines. Last fall, more than half the nation's governors declared their opposition to accepting Syrian refugees, saying a pause was needed until security concerns are addressed.

That sense of being shut out of decision-making reflects a wider distrust of the government in parts of the West, where federal policies involving land, water and endangered species often clash with energy, timber and grazing interests. Though the refugee debate is different, it exposes the same raw nerves among opponents, who also question the economic and social impact.

In a letter to her commissioners, Ravalli County resident Birte Nellessen said, "to fool ourselves that we are helping 'poor folks driven out of their homeland by war' is ridiculous. They openly and blazingly state that they are coming to destroy us and our culture. . . . Why we would spend any of our hard earned money on people like that?"

Nellessen, who moved to the U.S. from Germany 20 years ago, says officials should instead support local folks in need and that a smarter course would be to send supplies or money to help refugees rebuild in their homeland.

"I mean, what's a Syrian or Kenyan going to do in winter in Montana? Seriously."

The answer is coming. The International Rescue Committee has met with Missoula's mayor, police chief and others to prepare for the refugees—about 100 will come over a year's time. The agency plans to reopen a resettlement office here this fall, after a 25-year absence. Those most likely to be relocated include Congolese, Afghans and Syrians who will have no family ties, so they'll have to live within a 50-mile radius of the office.

Mary Poole is looking forward to their arrival.

About 750 people have signed up to help refugees make the transition, she says. One former Missoula resident now living in Mongolia wants to get involved when she returns.

Poole is already thinking ahead, too, about how this could change the life of her 17-month-old son, Jack.

She envisions a day, she says, when he "will be able to sit in a school next to someone of a different color, of a different language, of a different culture—and be able to learn that he lives in a global world. . . . I don't think we can be insulated anymore."

Poole knows resistance remains, and still meets with those who don't want refugees here. She says she's even made friends with some vocal opponents, recently inviting them to her house for a barbecue.

"We're asking for compassion," she says, "and must be able to give that ourselves."

Activist Mary Poole was haunted by the 2015 photo of a Syrian refugee boy washed ashore in Turkey. She asked: Why not bring a small number of Syrian families to Missoula? (AP Photo/Brennan Linsley)

And there's always a chance to win some over.

"They are us,' she says of the opponents. "They are part of our community, and in order for this to be as successful as it possibly can be, it's about being in it together."

Jefferson City, Missouri
Minorities missing in many legislatures

I was nearing completion of a project looking at whether a growing movement for redistricting reforms could help more minorities win election to state legislatures and Congress. My story draft included this fact from an analysis I did of U.S. Census Bureau data and legislative demographics: Whites who aren't Hispanic make up three-fifths of the U.S. population but still hold more than four-fifths of all congressional and state legislative seats.

That provided the pivot point for us to reshape the story into one of the early installments in the Divided America series. The new focus: Why do the people elected to represent Americans not reflect America's increasingly diverse demographics? And what effect does this have on how people view their place in the U.S.?

I expanded the data to drill down to the demographics of each of the more than 7,100 state and federal legislative districts. Among the findings: Some areas where Hispanics comprise more than 60, 75 or even 85 percent of the population are still represented by white lawmakers. Disparities also exist for other racial minority groups. Some incumbents in those districts declined or avoided repeated interview requests. But with the help of additional AP reporters, we went straight to the people living in those areas to get their thoughts about America's representative democracy. We also interviewed numerous pioneering minority lawmakers.

It all boiled down to this: Though there are many white lawmakers effectively representing minority communities, when the people elected don't look, think, talk or act like the people they represent, it can deepen divisions among us.

—David A. Lieb, AP State Government Reporter

* * *

As Virginia's only Latino state lawmaker, Alfonso Lopez made it his first order of business to push for a law granting in-state college tuition to immigrants living in the U.S. illegally since childhood.

The bill died in committee.

So Lopez tried again the next year. And the year after that.

Now, in his fifth year in office, Lopez is gearing up for one more attempt in 2017.

"If we had a more diverse (legislature) and more Latinos in the House of Delegates," he says, "I don't think it would be as difficult."

America's government is a lot whiter than American itself, and not just in Virginia.

While minorities have made some political gains in recent decades, they remain significantly underrepresented in Congress and nearly every state legislature though they comprise a growing share of the U.S. population, according to an analysis of demographic data by The Associated Press. The disparity in elected representation is especially large for Hispanics, even though they are now the nation's largest ethnic minority.

A lack of political representation can carry real-life consequences, and not only on hot-button immigration issues. State spending for public schools, housing and social programs all can have big implications for minority communities. So can decisions on issues such as criminal justice reform, election laws or the printing of public documents in other languages besides English.

When the people elected don't look, think, talk or act like the people they represent, it can deepen divisions that naturally exist in the U.S.

Campaigning door-to-door in the heavily Latino neighborhoods of south Omaha, Nebraska, first-time legislative candidate Tony Vargas has talked with numerous people afraid to participate in democracy. Some felt shunned or confused when they once attempted to vote. Others have misconceptions about the legal requirements to do so. Some simply believe their vote doesn't matter.

"You can hear the fear in people's voices, and you can hear that they feel like less of a member of society, less of an American," says Vargas, whose parents came to the U.S. from Peru.

Though Hispanics now make up 10 percent of Nebraska's population, there is not a single Latino lawmaker in its Legislature.

The Associated Press analyzed data from the U.S. Census Bureau, Congress and the National Conference of State Legislatures to determine

Tony Vargas, candidate for the Nebraska legislature, reaches out to a potential voter in Omaha, NE, June 12, 2016. (AP Photo/Nati Harnik)

the extent to which the nation's thousands of lawmakers match the demographics of its hundreds of millions of residents. The result: Non-Hispanic whites make up a little over 60 percent of the U.S. population, but still hold more than 80 percent of all congressional and state legislative seats. Among major minority groups:

— Blacks are the least underrepresented but still face sizable gaps in some places. In Mississippi and Louisiana, about one-third of the population is black. Yet each state has a single black member of Congress and a disproportionately small number in their state legislatures.
— More than half the states still have no lawmakers with Asian or Pacific Islander heritage, and just four states have any in Congress.
— Hispanics comprise more than 17 percent of the U.S. population, yet they are fewer than 7 percent in Congress and fewer than 4 percent of state legislators. The gaps in representation exist even in California, New Mexico and Texas, with the largest Latino populations.

There are many reasons for the disparities.

The U.S. Hispanic population generally is younger and less likely to be eligible voters. And those who can vote often don't. Voter turnout among Hispanics (as well as Asian Americans) dipped to just 27 percent in 2014, compared with 41 percent for blacks and 46 percent for whites, according to the Pew Research Center. Low voter involvement can make it harder to recruit minority candidates, and less likely for minority communities to be targeted by campaigns.

"It becomes sort of self-fulfilling—they're not likely voters, so you don't talk to them, and because you don't talk to them, they don't become likely voters," says political consultant Roger Salazar, whose clients include California's legislative Latino caucus.

The power of incumbency also can work against minority representation. Decades of deeply ingrained name recognition have helped white lawmakers continue to get elected in some districts where population shifts have gradually made racial minorities the majority.

Another factor is the way legislative districts have been drawn. Racial gerrymandering can occur either when minority communities are divided among multiple districts to dilute their voting strength or when they are packed heavily into a single district to diminish the likelihood of minorities winning multiple seats.

In states that have elected a critical mass of minority legislators, they've claimed some policy successes.

In California, a new law expands the state's Medi-Cal health care program for low-income residents to immigrant children, regardless of their legal status. The state budget includes $15 million for nonprofits to help immigrants gain U.S. citizenship or remain in the country. And a law that kicked in last year provided drivers' licenses to more than 600,000 people living in the country illegally.

But minority legislators in numerous states told the AP that their priorities have been stymied partly due to a lack of others like them.

For 22 years, Delaware state Sen. Margaret Rose Henry has been the only black senator in a state where African-Americans comprise more than

Delaware Gov. Jack Markell, right, stands with state legislators, from left, Rep. J.J. Johnson, Rep. Sean Lynn, Sen. Margaret Rose Henry, Sen. Brian Bushweller and Rep. Stephanie Bolden, after signing a House joint resolution that apologizes for the state's role in slavery, February 10, 2016. (AP Photo/ Steve Ruark, File)

one-fifth of all residents. Henry says she has long sought to improve the educational opportunities for black children bused under a Wilmington desegregation plan to suburban schools. But recommendations from multiple studies have gone nowhere over the years.

Now, a new commission has recommended realigning Wilmington area school districts and revising the state funding formula to direct more money to schools with larger numbers of students who are low-income, learning English or at high risk of not completing school. Henry fears the plan will again be difficult to pass.

"If there were more black elected officials, we would have a better chance to get something done," she says.

Constructing our own intellectual ghettos

For a reporter at The Associated Press, there's something depressing about researching the ways in which Americans are building their own news diets to shut out the voices of those who disagree with them. We live to expose people to worlds they don't know, not simply feed them facts that validate their own views. Inevitably, the rise of news outlets that cater to like-minded people makes us feel our work is more important than ever as an organization that seeks to gather people in a common town square.

You yearn for Americans to look up from their devices, to stop editing their social media feeds to eliminate "friends" who disagree with them. Seeing a presidential *campaign managed by an executive from a partisan news source seemed inevitable.*

In John Dearth and Peggy Albrecht, we found two people with keen interest in politics who rarely seek out the same news source. At the suggestion of my editor, we connected them in a telephone conversation. I didn't expect shouting — they were both too nice for that — but I did anticipate two people who would talk past each other instead of to each other

Yet that didn't happen. They listened to each other. No minds were changed, but they experienced someone who disagreed with them as a real person instead of a caricature. I chose to be encouraged by that, and by the record 84 million people who tuned in to see Hillary Clinton and Donald Trump on the same stage at the first presidential debate in the fall of 2016.

—David Bauder, AP Media Reporter

* * *

Meet Peggy Albrecht and John Dearth. Albrecht is a free-lance writer and comedian from Los Angeles who loved Bernie Sanders. Dearth, a retiree from Carmel, Indiana, grew up a Democrat but flipped with Ronald Reagan. He's a Trump guy.

They live in the same country, but as far as their news consumption goes, they might as well live on different planets.

Abrecht watches MSNBC's Rachel Maddow each night. She scans left-leaning websites Daily Kos, Talking Points Memo and Down With Tyranny, where recent headlines described Donald Trump as "pathetic" and "temperamentally unfit" to be president. She can read stories that describe Trump University as a scam and question whether the Republican candidate is as rich as he lets on. The website Think Progress, which has contrasted Trump's Republican endorsers with criticisms they've made of him, sends her email alerts.

Dearth is a fan of Fox Business Network anchors Neil Cavuto and Stuart Varney. He checks the Drudge Report, Town Hall and Heritage Foundation websites, where recent stories talked about Trump supporters being "terrorized" by demonstrators and suggested Hillary Clinton answered planted questions at a supposedly unscripted event. An American flag tangled in red tape illustrated a story about Obama administration business regulations.

Because of his internet search history, he's bombarded with solicitations to donate to conservative candidates and causes. The Democrats don't bother.

In a simpler time, Albrecht and Dearth might have gathered at a common television hearth to watch Walter Cronkite deliver the evening news.

But the growth in partisan media over the past two decades has enabled Americans to retreat into tribes of like-minded people who get news filtered through particular world views. Fox News Channel and Talking Points Memo thrive, with audiences that rarely intersect. What's big news in one world is ignored in another. Conspiracy theories sprout, anger abounds and the truth becomes ever more elusive.

Americans are becoming used to speaking at political opponents, and not with them. Prominent political observer Barack Obama is among those who have worried about the implications for democracy.

"Increasingly what happens is, we don't hear each other," the president said in a recent Fox News interview.

In this world of hundreds of channels and uncounted websites, of exquisitely targeted advertising and unbridled social media, it is easy to construct your own intellectual ghetto, however damaging that might be to the ideal of the free exchange of ideas.

"Right now the left plays to the left and the right plays to the right," said Glenn Beck, the former Fox News host who started TheBlaze, a conservative network, in 2010. "That's why we keep ratcheting up the heat. We're throwing red meat. We're in a room that is an echo chamber, and everybody's cheering."

Albrecht and Dearth don't rely exclusively on partisan media. Albrecht starts her day with the Los Angeles Times, and Dearth occasionally flips to MSNBC to hear opposing viewpoints, particularly on "Morning Joe."

That makes them typical: relatively few of the people who rely on opinionated news completely ignore the other side, said Kathleen Hall Jamieson, director of the Annenberg Public Policy Center at the University of Pennsylvania.

They do share mirrored misgivings about the major broadcast networks, newspapers and their related websites—the mainstream media.

"I don't call it mainstream," Albrecht said. "They don't give me points of view that I think are necessary to understand stories . . . I have to go to

Freelance writer and comedian Peggy Albrecht at her home in Westlake Village, CA, June 10, 2016. (AP Photo/Mark J. Terrill)

my liberal sites if I want to get a liberal point of view, other than my own."

"The so-called liberal media is not that at all," she said.

Dearth, meanwhile, avoids the evening newscasts on ABC, CBS and NBC because, "All three of them have a strong liberal slant on a lot of things."

That's the kind of thinking that inspired Roger Ailes to launch Fox News Channel in 1996. The former GOP operative mixed news during the day with a prime-time lineup that appealed to conservatives. The network's early slogans—"fair and balanced" and "we report, you decide"—were knowing nods to what mainstream outlets promise yet fail to achieve in the eyes of many conservative viewers like Dearth.

"It did reflect my views a lot more than any of the others," Dearth said. "It wasn't that I turned the others off, but I saw them much, much less."

By 2002, Fox had raced past CNN to become the top-rated news network.

This was the beginning of a golden age of partisan media, though Rush Limbaugh had started a boom of conservative talk radio in the early 1990s.

There wasn't anything to compare on the left, at least until summer 2006 when MSNBC host Keith Olbermann read about a speech where

Defense Secretary Donald Rumsfeld equated Iraq War opponents to pre-World War II appeasers. The next night, Olbermann angrily denounced Rumsfeld. Olbermann half-expected his boss to fire him, but management instead saw viewers had responded.

"The next day he came into my office and said, 'could you do one of those every night, buddy?'" Olbermann recalled.

His show became home for disaffected liberals in the Bush administration's final years. MSNBC hired Maddow and eventually made the entire network left-leaning. It didn't really stick: Low ratings forced a turn to straight news in daytime the last two years, but vestiges of partisanship remain.

Liberals like Jeff Cohen, communications professor at Ithaca College, believe that conservatives will always dominate mass media because of corporate ownership. That's less of an issue online; there, fueled by Fox's primacy and opposition to the war in Iraq, liberals began finding their voice in the early 2000s.

Writer Josh Marshall began blogging and reporting, developing the Talking Points Memo website. His work forced wider attention to issues like the firing of U.S. attorneys in the Bush administration, Republican voter suppression efforts and the fight against Social Security privatization. TPM has grown to 25 employees with offices in Washington and New York, with an average of 20 million page views a month.

Others followed Marshall's path, exposing readers like Albrecht to stories they might otherwise have not heard about.

Besides, she said, "I enjoy it more. It's always more fun to listen to people you happen to agree with."

Conservatives took advantage of new media, too. Georgia lawyer Erick Erickson became the best-known voice on the Red State site, which established itself with its quick advocacy against Bush's choice of Harriet Miers for the Supreme Court, whose nomination was withdrawn due to conservative opposition.

Breitbart, NewsMax, The Daily Caller and TheBlaze are other prominent online options on the right. Erickson recently sold Red State and started a new site, the Resurgent, and sees web outlets moving from simply informing readers to guiding them into political action.

We are left with fascinating parallel worlds.

Fox reports every December on a "War on Christmas," and Planned Parenthood is a huge target for right-wing media. Liberal organizations made Edward Snowden a hero and drummed against Pacific trade agreements. It took a while for the Flint water crisis to be noticed beyond the liberal press.

"I don't think it's as much a danger to democracy as people think it is," Olbermann said. "When the business changes to being all conservative media or all liberal media—though I don't know how that would happen—that's when it becomes dangerous."

Yet today's political media gets at least some of the blame for a hardening of attitudes. In his 2009 book, "Going to Extremes: How Like Minds Unite and Divide," Harvard University's Cass Sunstein argued that when like-minded people gather in groups, they tend to become more extreme in their views.

A generation ago, majorities in each political party described themselves as moderate. That's changed. In ABC News exit polling between 1976 and 1992, the number of Democrats who described themselves as liberal fluctuated between 24 to 34 percent. This year, 62 percent of the Democratic primary electorate said they were liberal. Similarly, 76 percent of today's Republicans identify themselves as conservative, roughly double what it was in the 1970s.

Social media amplifies political isolationism, because people are likely to spread information to people who agree with them, said Penn's Jamieson.

Who are you going to believe: the link you get from a trusted friend, or a mainstream media source that tells you the article is bunk?

Marty Baron, executive editor of The Washington Post, spoke with some distress this spring at the commencement of Temple University's School of Media and Communication.

"Today we are not so much communicating as miscommunicating," he said. "Or failing to communicate. Or choosing to communicate only with those who think as we do. Or communicating in a manner that is wholly detached from reality. Too often we look only for affirmation of our own ideas rather than opening ourselves to the ideas of others."

That thought was on Beck's mind when he had lunch a year ago with Arianna Huffington, founder of the left-leaning news site that bears her name. They talked about the need for an outlet where a conservative can talk about ideas to a liberal audience and vice versa.

"Let's try to make the case that a story matters to people who don't agree with me," he said. "Because my language would change, my approach would change. Things will be ratcheted down. We'll be able to understand each other again. I think there's a real need in the country for that."

For now, nothing's come of the idea.

So we tried it ourselves on a small scale. Peggy Albrecht, meet John Dearth. John, here's Peggy. We set up a conference call to let them do something they rarely have a chance to anymore: carry on a conversation with someone who's a polar opposite politically.

So what political position held by the other side most baffles them?

For Albrecht, it's the effort in some Republican-led states to require IDs to vote. She understands the political motivations—Republicans want to depress Democratic turnout—but doesn't fathom why the greater good of having as many Americans as possible vote doesn't prevail.

"I'm on the other side of it, to some extent," Dearth said. "I believe that everyone who is legal should be allowed to vote, I agree with that . . . What I do have a problem is that I'd like to make sure that people are legally able to vote."

How do they feel about Barack Obama?

John Dearth on his pickup truck outside his home in Carmel, IN, June 13, 2016. (AP Photo/Michael Conroy)

"I think he's overreached with his executive actions and so forth," Dearth said. "I believe that the country is not as well off. Don't get me wrong, I know he came in during a tough time, but I don't think he's made the country better."

Albrecht, meanwhile, thinks he hasn't been liberal enough.

"Overall, yes, I like him, but I don't agree with everything he says," she said. "I find a lot of Democrats believe that, but sometimes when I say it I'll get attacked—'you're not a real Democrat.' I am, actually."

Said Dearth: "I hear that from my side, too—people who say if you don't agree with this, you can't be a real conservative. That goes both ways."

Dearth voted for Ted Cruz in the Indiana Republican primary, but he's on board with Trump. Albrecht hasn't decided whether to support Hillary Clinton in the fall. "I will never vote for Trump—on so many levels," she said, and began to list several reasons.

"What Peggy says about Trump, I could probably echo the same things about Hillary," Dearth said. "There are a lot of untruths. Maybe that's just the way it is. I think the pot calling the kettle black is probably happening on both sides."

Unfailingly polite, Albrecht and Dearth talked politics for nearly an hour without raising their voices. They agreed on the need for more investigative reporting from the media. The discussion left Dearth nostalgic for a time when "we had people of different parties get together, go out to have a drink together. We don't seem to have that anymore."

"I know," Albrecht said. "The camaraderie has disappeared in favor of taking sides and outdoing one another. It helps to co-mingle and get to hear people as people. Here Jack and I are talking and we have different viewpoints—completely different viewpoints on some things and similar on others. And look at that, nobody got murdered."

Memphis, Tennessee

Rosy economic averages bypass many in US

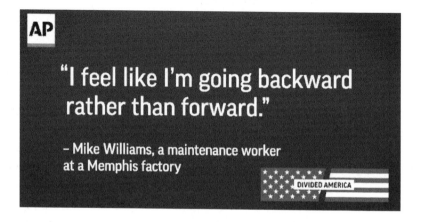

The idea behind this story emerged as the economy seemed to be improving at a faster pace in 2015 and 2016, but many Americans insisted they were seeing little progress. The disconnect was apparent in interviews I conducted and Twitter interactions, as well as in polls, and most obviously in the tumultuous primaries in both political parties in the spring of 2016.

Income inequality was also a top economic and political issue, and it seemed to point the way to an answer: Average economic data, such as incomes and wealth, were increasingly lifted by the very wealthy and less reflective of what the typical American was experiencing. In wonky terms, the average was pulling ahead of the median, making it less meaningful.

This was also happening geographically: Economists regularly cited about 25-30 large cities as hot spots for job and income growth, including Dallas, Seattle, Denver, San

Francisco, Austin, Tex., and others. Yet a much larger number were stumbling along. One of those places was Memphis, which enjoyed economic growth closer to the national average in the 1990s but had since, particularly after the Great Recession, fallen behind. It turned out to be ripe territory for illustrating the trend.
—Chris Rugaber, AP Economics Writer

* * *

Dozens of FedEx jets queue up for takeoff at the airport here. Beale Street, the heart of the music district, hums with tourists. Yet the empty storefronts in Memphis' moribund downtown and the cash-advance shops strewn near its highways tell another story.

It's a tale of two cities, all in one place. And it's a tale of two Americas: the one that national averages indicate has all but recovered from the Great Recession and the one lost in the statistics.

The pattern is evident in cities and towns across America, from Memphis to Colorado Springs, Colorado, from Wichita to Jacksonville: The national numbers aren't capturing the experience of many typical people in typical communities.

A key reason is that pay and wealth are flowing disproportionately to the rich, skewing the data used to measure economic health—and producing an economy on paper that most Americans don't recognize in their own lives. That disconnect has fueled much of the frustration and anxiety that have propelled the insurgent presidential campaigns of Donald Trump and Bernie Sanders.

Again and again, primary voters who were most worried about the economy told pollsters that they had cast their ballots for Trump or Sanders, according to Edison Research, which conducted the surveys on behalf of The Associated Press and television networks.

Trump's candidacy, in particular, has been driven by support in some of the most economically distressed regions in the country, where jobs have been automated, eliminated, or moved to other states and countries. It's in these places that the outsider message of an unconventional candidate promising a return to the way things used to be resonates most.

Mike Williams voted for Trump in Tennessee's March primary, which the billionaire won easily. To many, it would seem that Williams is doing pretty

A pedestrian walks past an empty storefront in Memphis, TN, June 1, 2016 (AP Photo/Karen Pulfer Focht)

well—he earns $22 an hour as a maintenance worker at an Owens-Corning factory, along with health care and retirement benefits. But his hourly pay has only recently returned to where it was a decade ago, when he worked as a welder.

"I feel like I'm going backward rather than forward," Williams, 51, said on a recent afternoon after finishing his shift.

One reason he backed Trump, he said, is that he feels less secure than in the past, when more manufacturing work was available.

"I remember when you could quit a job today and go to work somewhere else tomorrow," Williams said. "There was always someone hiring."

The depth of that kind of insecurity after seven years of national economic expansion has caught many observers off guard.

"The political reaction to the economy leads me to wonder if we're looking at the wrong things," said Carl Tannenbaum, chief economist at Northern Trust and former economist at the Federal Reserve. "The averages certainly don't tell the whole story."

Consider incomes for the average U.S. household. They ticked up 0.7 percent from 2008 to 2014, after taking inflation into account. But even that scant increase reflected mainly the rise in income for the richest tenth of households, which pulled up the average. For most others, incomes actually decreased—as much as 6 percent for the bottom 20 percent, at a time when the economy was mostly recovering.

Or consider employment. The U.S. economy has added a healthy average of roughly 200,000 jobs a month since 2011. Yet most have been either high-paying or low-paying positions. By the end of 2015, the nation still had fewer middle-income jobs than it did before the recession, according to the Georgetown University Center on Education and the Workforce.

That reflects what economists call the "hollowing out" of the workforce, as traditional mid-level positions such as office administrators, bookkeepers, and factory assembly-line workers are cut in recessions and never fully recover their previous levels of employment.

An empty business sign on Elvis Presley Boulevard. Many of the new jobs, in Memphis and elsewhere, are in lower-paying industries and more likely to be part time or temporary. (AP Photo/Karen Pulfer Focht)

Part-time jobs surged in the recession, too, and remained high in the recovery, even while full-time work was slower to return. The number of full-time jobs has risen just 1.3 percent since December 2007, when the recession officially began. Part-time positions are up more than 12 percent.

In Memphis, hiring resumed after the recession and the unemployment rate has dropped to match the national figure of 5 percent. But jobs in low-paying industries, such as retail, restaurants and hotels, are the only category to have fully recovered from the recession, according to Moody's Analytics. Higher- and middle-paying jobs still trail their pre-recession levels.

In Millington, a Memphis suburb where Trump held a rally in February at a military airfield, residents complain that most of the available jobs are in the fast-food chains that dot Highway 51, the main thoroughfare.

The rebound from the recession has been felt in vastly different ways not only by income levels but across geographic lines. Areas like Las Vegas that still bear deep scars from the housing crisis have lagged behind the nation's recovery. So have cities like Memphis that need robust consumer spending to fuel growth at the shipping and logistics firms that form the backbone of its economy.

By contrast, cities like Seattle, Denver and Austin, Texas, with heavy concentrations of information technology, management consulting or other highly paid services, have enjoyed a disproportionate share of the job and income growth.

In other words, the richest places in the country are making the economy look better than it actually is, while places like Memphis stagnate.

In the first half of the recovery, jobs grew 5.6 percent nationwide. Yet in the wealthiest one-fifth of zip codes, hiring jumped 11.2 percent, according to the Economic Innovation Group think tank. For the rest of the country, total jobs increased just 3.3 percent.

"It's hard to find an average city," Tannenbaum says. "There just aren't a whole lot right in the middle."

The same is true for households. These data suggest that the post-World War II trend of a steadily growing middle class, lifted by broader national prosperity, is reversing.

Slightly fewer than half of American adults now fall in the middle-class camp, according to the Pew Research Center, a vast shift. In 1971, 61 percent of households were middle class, according to Pew, which defines middle class as income between two-thirds and double the median household income.

And while home prices have risen nationwide since 2012, they're still below their boom-era levels in most parts of the country. Since most middle-class wealth is in home equity, those families are poorer than they were before the recession.

By and large, more affluent Americans are the ones who hold stock—and stock prices are back near record heights.

In Las Vegas, which is still recovering from its huge housing boom and bust, Tracy Brigida's husband, Michael, last summer lost his second job in three years. Tracy, 48, has been paying the bills by substitute-teaching while raising their two children, one of whom is autistic and is home-schooled.

They still owe more on their Las Vegas home than it's worth, having bought it nine years ago. They hoped it would build wealth for their retirements. Now, it's a money pit.

The couple initially supported Wisconsin Gov. Scott Walker's presidential campaign. But after Michael's latest layoff, they switched to Trump.

Families like hers, she says, seem forgotten in the celebration of rosy national economic averages.

"This administration wants to tell us the economy is better and people are getting jobs," she said. "But that's not my experience."

With higher-paying jobs clustering in wealthier metro areas, business and political leaders in the weaker cities fight to attract and retain employers. Memphis has provided tax breaks to attract or keep 36 companies, including Electrolux, Mitsubishi Electric and Unilever.

Community leaders have also focused on improving the education and skills of the area's workforce, which trail national averages. A Brookings Institution analysis found that three-quarters of jobs in Memphis require post-high school education or training—something that 40 percent of the area's adults lack.

Rising automation at many warehouses is also undercutting efforts to create solid middle-income jobs. Memphis is a leading transport hub: In addition to FedEx, shipping firms such as UPS, DHL, and XPO Logistics have warehouses in the region. So do other companies like Nike. Yet

Memphis still has 3,200 fewer transportation and warehousing jobs than it did before the recession.

Contributing also to the decline of middle-income positions has been the rising use of temporary workers, whose ranks have surged 54 percent in Memphis since the recession ended while the area's overall jobs grew just 3.3 percent. City officials involved in workforce training say some of the unemployed have 25 years of work history—all of it through temp firms.

Chris Rice, 29, has worked steadily in the Memphis region for the past 10 years, all at temporary jobs. Rice most recently worked as a forklift driver for Electrolux and for CEVA Logistics, a privately held warehouse and distribution firm.

The CEVA job ended after the company lost a contract to distribute Microsoft's X-Box, Rice said during a job fair at a community center in Bartlett, a Memphis suburb.

Rice said he was hopeful of getting a new temp job at an assembly plant owned by printer manufacturer Brother International. He was the only forklift driver at the job fair.

Still, "I'd love to have a permanent job," he said. "I'm tired of going from temp agency to temp agency when there's no work."

Orlando, Florida
Gun views fractious even as fewer bear arms

There's a sorrowful litany in this country of places marked by the pain and blood-shed of mass death: Columbine and Sandy Hook, Blacksburg and Fort Hood, San Bernardino and Aurora. Just before this assignment came my way, we added a new entry, Orlando.

It would be easy to dismiss the list as simply a sorrowful fact of life in America, where guns are plentiful and often beloved and the debate over controlling the weapons about as polarized as you can get. It became clear soon into reporting this piece, though, that it wasn't always this way.

43

I sat down with some of our data experts to look at the available data and see if we could draw any conclusions on how things had changed and the facts were surprising: Not only huge shifts in how people felt about guns, but a notable change in how many people chose to own them. Paired with other reporting, we learned how the change in public opinion dovetailed with shifting legal interpretation of gun laws and the growing influence of the gun lobby.

It's hard to imagine now, but within many Americans' lifetimes, there was a span when views on guns were so different and multiple-casualty shootings weren't part of the drumbeat of daily life. How we got from that point to now is a fascinating study in politics, lobbying and fear.

—Matt Sedensky, AP National Writer

* * *

Look anywhere in this nation born of a bloody revolution of musket fire, and you're likely to find sharp disagreement over guns.

Democrats war with Republicans; small towns are pitted against cities. Women and men are at odds, as are blacks and whites and old and young. North clashes with South, East with West.

"The current gun debate is more polarized and sour than any time before in American history," said Adam Winkler, a constitutional law professor at UCLA and author of the 2011 book, "Gunfight: The Battle Over the Right to Bear Arms in America."

Still numb from the latest mass shooting, in Orlando, it's easy to imagine that guns have always divided us this way. But a close look at survey data over decades shows they haven't.

There was a time when most citizens favored banning handguns, the chief gun lobbyists supported firearm restrictions, and courts hadn't yet interpreted the Second Amendment as guaranteeing a personal right to bear arms for self-defense at home.

Today, in a country of hundreds of millions of guns, public opinion and interpretation of the law have shifted so much that outright gun bans are unthinkable. It's true that large segments of the public have expressed support for some aspects of gun regulation—but when Americans have been asked to say which is more important, gun control or gun rights, they trend toward the latter.

That shift has come, perhaps surprisingly, as fewer Americans today choose to keep a gun in their home. The General Social Survey by NORC at the University of Chicago—one of the foremost authorities on gun ownership—found 31 percent of households had guns in 2014, down from a high of 50.4 percent in 1977.

"Institutions have repeated, 'More guns, less crime. More guns, less crime,' over and over again for almost 40 years, and it's hard to turn that belief around in any easy way," said Joan Burbick, an emeritus professor at Washington State University who wrote "Gun Show Nation: Gun Culture and American Democracy" and who owns a gun for hobby shooting.

Among the longest-existing measures of public gun sentiment is a Gallup poll question asking whether there should be a law banning handguns except by police and other authorized people. When it was first asked, in July 1959, 60 percent of respondents approved of such a measure.

By last October, only 27 percent agreed.

NRA President Charlton Heston holds up a rifle as he addresses gun owners during a "get-out-the-vote" rally in Manchester, NH, October 21, 2002. (AP Photo/Jim Cole)

Many point to a single date as crucial in the societal shift: May 21, 1977, when a contingent of National Rifle Association members staged a revolt that remade the group's leadership, scuttled plans for a retreat from politics and sealed a rightward, hard-line shift. It led to a fundamental remaking of the NRA, which had come to accept some gun laws, including the Gun Control Act of 1968.

"That was the moment, in one evening, when the gun debate in America radically changed," said Winkler.

The gun lobby's increasingly powerful voice found receptive ears among a public left uneasy by civil rights battles, assassinations and growing urban lawlessness. Over time, statehouses and Congress bowed to the influence of the NRA and its allies. And in 2008, the U.S. Supreme Court finally declared Americans have the right to a gun for self-defense.

"What they (gun rights advocates) did is a classic example of how you make constitutional change: They realized they needed to win in the court of public opinion before you could win in the court of law," said Michael Waldman, president of the Brennan Center for Justice at New York University and author of "The Second Amendment: A Biography."

The NRA did not respond to an interview request. But data from the GSS and the Pew Research Center offers a sketch of what the gun-owning populace looks like today: Overwhelmingly white and male, concentrated in rural areas, and more often identifying with or leaning toward the Republican Party. They also have higher incomes and are more likely to vote.

Though polarization appears in broad questions on gun rights, far more consensus emerges on individual proposals.

A Pew poll released in August showed 85 percent of people support background checks for purchases at gun shows and in private sales; 79 percent support laws to prevent the mentally ill from buying guns; 70 percent approve of a federal database to track gun sales; and 57 percent favor a ban on assault weapons.

"The fact is it's not divisive. The things that we're advocating in the American public, when you're talking about keeping guns out of dangerous hands, we all agree," said Dan Gross, president of the Brady Campaign to Prevent Gun Violence. "The only place where this is truly a controversial issue is, tragically and disgracefully, in Congress and in our statehouses across the country."

Rocky Ford, Colorado
Town and country offer differing realities

The Trump phenomenon surprised a lot of experts, liberal and conservative alike. What these experts typically had in common is that, regardless of their political leanings, they lived in urban areas.

Trump's core message of a country that's left you behind, an alien place and a confusing culture that symbolizes the victory of foreigners, makes sense in rural America. It's a part of the country that often gets overlooked by urbanites worried about their own, all-too-real struggles with income inequality, growth and housing costs. Those are the issues that have dominated political debate during the Obama years among urban elites. But there are plenty of voters who don't have those concerns.

My home base of Colorado was the perfect place to look at those two contrasting worlds. Despite Colorado's stereotypes, it is one of the more urbanized states in the country. The newly booming Denver metro area is home to an increasing amount of harried professionals whose complaints mirror those of people in Eastern metro areas. That leaves Colorado's rural areas feeling increasingly left behind, resentful, and ready for Trump.

—Nicholas Riccardi, AP Western Political Writer

* * *

Peggy Sheahan's rural Otero County is steadily losing population. Middle-class jobs vanished years ago as pickling and packing plants closed. She's had to cut back on her business repairing broken windshields to help nurse her husband after a series of farm accidents, culminating in his breaking his neck falling from a bale of hay.

She collects newspaper clippings on stabbings and killings in the area—one woman's body was found in a field near Sheahan's farm—as heroin use rises.

"We are so worse off, it's unbelievable," said Sheahan, 65, who plans to vote for Donald Trump.

In Denver, 175 miles to the northwest, things are going better for Andrea Pacheco. Thanks to the Supreme Court, the 36-year-old could finally marry her partner, Jen Winters, in June. After months navigating Denver's superheated housing market, they snapped up a bungalow at the edge of town. Pacheco supports Hillary Clinton to build on President Barack Obama's legacy.

"There's a lot of positive things that happened—obviously the upswing in the economy," said Pacheco, a 36-year-old fundraiser for nonprofits. "We were in a pretty rough place when he started out and I don't know anyone who isn't better off eight years later."

There are few divides in the United States greater than that between rural and urban places. Town and country represent not just the poles of the nation's two political parties, but different economic realities that are transforming the 2016 presidential election.

Cities are trending Democratic and are on an upward economic shift, with growing populations and rising property values. Rural areas are

New apartment buildings line a street in trendy downtown Denver. The city's current success contrasts the economic slump that often defines life in rural Colorado. (AP Photo/Brennan Linsley)

increasingly Republican, shedding population and suffering economically as commodity and energy prices drop.

"The urban-rural split this year is larger than anything we've ever seen," said Scott Reed, a political strategist for the U.S. Chamber of Commerce who has advised previous GOP campaigns.

While plenty of cities still struggle with endemic poverty and joblessness, a report from the Washington-based Economic Innovation Group found that half of new business growth in the past four years has been concentrated in 20 populous counties.

"More and more economic activity is happening in cities as we move to higher-value services playing a bigger role in the economy," said Ross Devol, chief researcher at the Milken Institute, an independent economic think tank. "As economies advance, economic activity just tends to concentrate in fewer and fewer places."

That concentration has brought a whole host of new urban problems—rising inequality, traffic and worries that the basics of city life are increasingly out of the reach of the middle class. Those fears inform

Democrats' emphasis on income inequality, wages and pay equity in contrast to the general anxiety about economic collapse that comes from Republicans who represent an increasingly desperate rural America.

These two different economic worlds are writ large in Colorado. It is among the states with the greatest economic gap between urban and rural areas, according to an Associated Press review of EIG data.

The state's sprawling metropolitan areas from Denver to Colorado Springs is known as the Front Range. As it has grown to include nearly 90 percent of the state's population, it has trended Democratic. Rural areas, which have become more Republican, resent Denver's clout. In 2013, a rural swath of the state unsuccessfully tried to secede to create its own state of Northern Colorado after the Democratic-controlled statehouse passed new gun control measures and required rural areas to use renewably generated electricity.

Denver City Councilman Rafael Espinoza has seen his neighborhood of modest bungalows occupied by largely Latino families abruptly transformed into a collection of condominiums housing affluent professionals. (AP Photo/ Brennan Linsley)

In Denver, City Councilman Rafael Espinoza was elected last year as part of a group of candidates questioning the value of Denver's runaway growth.

Espinoza has seen his neighborhood of modest bungalows occupied by largely Latino families transformed into a collection of condominiums housing affluent professionals.

"Money just drives the discussion. In the presidential, Bernie Sanders was my guy for that one reason," Espinoza said.

In contrast, Bill Hendren is desperate for money. He has about $4 in coins in a plastic cup he keeps in the cottage on a small farm where he lives, rent-free. Hendren's truck was stolen 18 months ago and he was unable to travel to perform the odd jobs in Otero County that kept him afloat. He's now functionally homeless and a Trump backer.

"I don't ever see a president caring about anyone who's living paycheck to paycheck—if they did they'd have put the construction people back to work," Hendren said. "Trump's got the elite scared because he doesn't belong to them."

Bill Hendren tends to goats on the property of a landowner who is allowing him to stay rent-free for a year in exchange for work, outside Manzanola, CO, July 1, 2016 (AP Photo/Brennan Linsley)

If bad luck and geography conspired to impoverish Bill Hendren, it's an excess of money that's to blame for Robin Sam's plight. Sam, 62, left one apartment counting on moving into another one being built in the rapidly-gentrifying and historically black neighborhood where he grew up. But that facility raised its rent over the threshold of Sam's $1,055 Section 8 voucher, and he's been living in a homeless shelter all year, unable to find a new place in Denver's fiercely competitive housing market.

"I feel like I'm being pushed out," said Sam, who is black. He recalls houses and apartments being barred to blacks in his youth decades ago, but senses something else at play now.

"It's money—and money changes everything," he said.

Staten Island, New York
Bridging the gap between police, policed

Staten Island is just a few miles across New York Harbor from Manhattan, even closer to Brooklyn. But many New Yorkers never set foot there and Staten Islanders chafe at being "forgotten." So when we set out to get a handle on police-community relations on the island two years after a black man, Eric Garner, died in a confrontation with cops, I wasn't sure what to expect. It was hardly a subject likely to engender warm and fuzzy feelings toward an outsider.

Indeed, it didn't always go smoothly. Stopped at night in a public housing project by a white reporter, residents, nearly all of them black, spoke thoughtfully, but none would give their names. Some of the borough's many retired cops were candid in speaking about the challenges of the job and lamented racial tensions, but others shied from questions and current officers wouldn't talk without departmental permission. AP photographer Seth Wenig, my reporting partner, tried to intervene when he saw a man hitting a woman on a street corner one night and ended up bruised and relieved of his cameras.

But many people were generous in sharing their island. Leroy Downs, who joined a suit against the NYPD over stop-and-frisk, spent hours driving me around his neighborhood of roller-coaster hills. We ended the night with a late meal in one of the north shore's Sri Lankan restaurants, a side of his home turf he'd never known before. Rich Bruno, the neighborhood's former top cop, was initially skeptical of a request to meet, but ended up taking me on a five hour tour of the North Shore, narrated from a policing point-of-view. If their points of view frequently diverged, they at least agreed on this much _ even as the police and the policed struggle to recast their relationship, they have little choice but to coexist.

—Adam Geller, AP National Writer

* * *

On an unusually cool night for summer, Mike Perry and his crew thread the sidewalks running through Staten Island's Stapleton Houses, tracked by police cameras bolted to the apartment blocks and positioned atop poles.

"The better the weather, the more people will be out," Perry says. "Activity—not all good, neither."

Perry's group, five black men and one Latino, all acknowledge past crimes or prison time. Perry, himself, used to deal drugs around another low-income housing complex, two miles away. Now, though, their Cure Violence team works to defuse arguments that can lead to shootings and match people with job training and counseling. Their goals are not so different from those of the police.

While Perry gives cops their due, he keeps his distance. Two years ago, within walking distance of this spot, a black man named Eric Garner died in a confrontation with police officers. Garner was suspected of selling loose cigarettes; an officer wrestled him to the ground by his neck. His last words—"I can't breathe"—were captured on cellphone video that rocketed across the internet.

"I know those officers did not mean to kill Eric," says Perry, a 37-year-old father of two who knew Garner.

But, "you need to look an officer in the eye who doesn't understand and go, 'Brother, I want to get home, too.' They're defending these communities that they don't know."

As Americans struggle with the highly publicized deaths of black men in encounters with police in Minnesota, Louisiana and across the country, and now the sniper killing of five Dallas officers, Perry and his fellow Staten Islanders have the dubious distinction of being a step ahead. Since Garner's death in July 2014, they have confronted a measure of the anger, pain and alienation that the nation now shares. On this 58-square-mile island that residents say often feels like a small town though it's part of the nation's biggest city, police and the policed have had to coexist.

The events of recent weeks have focused new attention on the chasm between police and minorities, one of so many divides in this contentious election year. Years of tension have left people wary in both the policing community and in minority neighborhoods, with many yearning for one another's respect.

A memorial at the site of Eric Garner's death in Staten Island, NY. The 43-year-old black man died in July 2014 after a white police officer placed him in a chokehold during an arrest for selling loose cigarettes. (AP Photo/ Seth Wenig)

* * *

It's not simple, though, to change the way people see each other. "What we have to bear in mind is that when a particular culture has been created, or when people sense a certain culture is operating, it takes time in order to change that culture," says the Rev. Victor Brown, a pastor of one of the larger African-American churches on Staten Island's North Shore. Brown, a spiritual adviser to Garner's family who criticized the grand jury's decision not to indict the officer involved, serves as a part-time police chaplain.

The challenge was captured in a nationwide poll last summer by the Associated Press-NORC Center for Public Affairs, in which 81 percent of black Americans said police are too quick to use deadly force, compared with 33 percent of whites. A third of blacks said they trust police to work in the best interest of the community, less than half the percentage of whites.

The voices of Staten Islanders speak to attitudes and experience that are often more complicated than might be reflected in polling numbers.

Like the white retired officer who credits a longtime black partner for much of his success in patrolling poor neighborhoods, and worries today's cops are not street-wise enough.

Or the black street vendor who rails against police for Garner's death, but says officers are needed to clean up the street where that death occurred.

"I think the divide is worse than it should be and more than people think it is," says Joe Brandefine, a retired NYPD detective who helped organize a 2014 pro-police rally. "I believe there's truth in both sides, that each side needs to see each other in a little different light."

On Staten Island, police-community relationships have long been personal.

About 3,000 police officers, scores of retired cops and their families live here, many in the heavily white neighborhoods on the southern two-thirds of the island. In those neighborhoods, protests that followed Garner's death in July 2014 were met with "God Bless the NYPD" yard signs and pro-police rallies. The tensions intensified after a grand jury decided in late 2014 not to indict the officer for Garner's death. Two weeks later, a man claiming vengeance killed two police officers in Brooklyn, one of them a former Staten Island school safety officer.

"As far as Staten Islanders are concerned, the police are family and I think it's like standing by your family no matter what," says Samantha Smith, whose father, grandfather and uncle all worked as officers and who is writing a book about 9/11's impact on the island's first responder households.

On an island of 475,000 that is 75 percent white and mostly suburban, the North Shore's comparatively dense neighborhoods are home to nearly all of the borough's African-Americans, enclaves of Liberian, Mexican, and Sri Lankan immigrants.

Five miles of water divide Staten Island from Manhattan's southern tip and you can't get here by subway. That separation from the rest of the city has long united islanders—not just the ferry ride or detested bridge tolls, but also conservative politics and a shared sense that their borough is ignored.

Spend your life here and it can feel like you know everybody, residents say, recalling how they aided each other after Superstorm Sandy. But very few blacks live below the Staten Island Expressway, which some residents say amounts to a local Mason-Dixon line, reinforcing divisions of race and economics that shade the tensions around policing.

Richard Bruno, 54, is the former commanding office of Staten Island's 120th Precinct, and lives in one of the precinct's largely white neighborhoods. But he belies the stereotype of the white cop uninitiated to life in poor neighborhoods.

"I grew up in a tenement until I was 7 years old," says Bruno, whose father, a truck driver, eventually saved $3,000 for a deposit on a house on Staten Island. "I remember for sport, shooting with dart guns the cockroaches off the wall . . . I think that gave me an extra sense of empathy for people that have to live like that."

On this overcast June morning, Bruno, who retired from the force at the end of 2007, points to places where police intervention worked. Here's the corner off Richmond Terrace where officers caught a notorious graffiti artist. He nods to the church where he met with Mexican immigrants, many in the country illegally, trying to gain trust needed to curb a series of robberies and attacks.

"The good thing about being able to keep these communities safe is because they were isolated pockets, you could focus your resources," he says. "Now to some citizens, maybe that might feel like that's an occupation, while other citizens that live in the communities welcome it. We found mostly, overwhelmingly, they welcomed it."

But Bruno, who followed an older brother into the NYPD, laments policing's blunt realities. Driving around the Stapleton Houses, he points to where a gunman dumped a car in 2003 after killing two undercover detectives.

He declines to pass judgment about Garner's death: "He wasn't an evil person. He was just out there hustling."

But in a city of 8.5 million and 35,000 cops, there will always be unintended casualties, Bruno says. That guarantees police will come in for resentment.

"You can't take anything personal, because it's not really about you at all. It's more about your position and anti-government," he says. "The public doesn't know any police officer personally. It's just really what they represent."

With the car windows open to the night air, Leroy Downs cruises past brick apartments and porch-front houses set into the slope rising from the ferry landing.

An eastern European couple, both white, shouts back greetings from steps across the street.

A group of black teens and young men welcome him in to their basketball game in a hilltop playground.

Downs, 41, has lived on Staten Island since he was 5 and works as a drug treatment counselor nearby. But tonight he talks about, just maybe, becoming a cop. It's not hard to imagine, given his almost paternal attention to the neighborhood. Except that Downs, who is black, has gone to court to fight the NYPD, and its widespread stop-and-frisks, mostly of black and Hispanic men.

He nears a spot where the hill starts dropping toward Jersey Street, known for random shooting.

"That's where we (Downs and his cousin) were parked when the officers pulled up on us when we were eating Wendy's. Just drove up and jumped out," he says. "It's like, bro, why is it like this? It's so frustrating."

It wasn't the first time. In 2000, police arrested Downs on the street, before moving on to nearby neighborhoods to pick up two men he says he'd never met, and accused the trio of conspiring to sell drugs. Downs' charges were eventually dismissed.

In 2011, Downs was sitting on his doorstep, talking on the phone, when two officers stopped to ask if he'd been smoking marijuana. A few weeks ago, a cop blocked his exit from a bank drive-thru lot to ask what he was doing there. He's hardly alone.

Shawn Mitchell, 28 and black, takes a break from a basketball game to recount being stopped recently by a police officer suspicious of his fast-food cup of lemonade.

"I feel like the tactics they're using as officers is we're the enemy," says Mitchell, who works odd jobs in construction. "Treat the badge like a badge used for respect, not for authority."

Down the hill, Darrell Pittard lifts his head from under the hood of a car he's repairing.

"This is Staten Island. You know what the pretext (for a police stop) is? Driving while black," says Pittard, 48, a subway mechanic who says he is

Leroy Downs, who has gone to court to fight the NYPD, and its widespread stop-and-frisks of mostly black and Hispanic men, plays basketball with local kids in the Staten Island, NY, May 25, 2016. (AP Photo/Seth Wenig)

frequently stopped by police who appear suspicious of a black man driving a Mercedes. "Granted, the engine is a little loud, OK. But here comes this guy on a Harley, what about him?"

Downs testified against the NYPD when a legal advocacy group sued and won a 2013 ruling that sweeping stop-and-frisks violate the constitutional rights of minority New Yorkers.

He sees little change in the relationship between cops and minorities despite the verdict. But he hasn't given up hoping.

"I can't imagine the world without police," he says. "It'd be anarchy."

It's been years since Larry Ambrosino was assistant principal of Police Officer Rocco Laurie Intermediate School 72. But as he walks the hallway, teachers offer handshakes and hugs to a man who's never really left.

For five decades, Ambrosino has worked to maintain this school, not far from the Staten Island Mall, as a living memorial to a slain New York cop. Laurie, raised on the island, was 23 in 1972 when he and partner Gregory Foster were shot in the back by members of the Black Liberation Army while policing Manhattan's Lower East Side.

"We do a lot of things to keep his name alive and let people know this is the kind of person we should look up to," says Ambrosino, a boyhood friend of Laurie's. "And there's a lot of cops out there today like Rocco, doing their job every day, and not sure if they're going to come home."

In another city, a dead cop might have faded from memory. Here, every sixth grader writes a research paper about Laurie. In March, 400 packed the gym for the 45th annual Laurie charity basketball game.

"A lot of kids in this school have parents who are police officers—a lot," says Peter Macellari, principal of the school, where about a quarter of the students are Hispanic and 5 percent are black. He notes that Rafael Ramos, one of the two cops shot to death in Brooklyn was once the school's security officer.

Laurie is hardly the only testament to islanders' regard for police.

Anthony Sabbatino, a former police officer who is now a firefighter, paid tribute with the recently closed 10-4 Bar & Grill, hiring an artist to paint a mural of first responders at the World Trade Center. When the president of the city teachers union joined activist Al Sharpton in a march, Staten Island teachers urged colleagues to protest by wearing blue to work.

"There's always going to be a couple of crazy cops that are wrong," said Ken Peterson, a retired NYPD detective who organized a 2014 pro-police rally that drew 700 to a South Shore park. "I just said this is ridiculous. They just don't even get respect, no less accolades for what they do."

Peterson acknowledges, though, that a rift remains.

Ambrosino has his own answer. Each year he tells Laurie students the story of their school's namesake, noting that Laurie was white and the partner slain alongside him was black.

"I always tell kids when Rocco Laurie and Gregory Foster were lying on the ground dying, they bled the same color blood."

The reminiscences, aided by cold beer, fill the Knights of Columbus hall on Staten Island's southeast shore even before the pledge to the flag.

Here's Pat Lavin, who can trace policing lineage from his grandfather's days as a bobby in northern England to his own son's promotion to detective in Brooklyn. Jack Hellman recalls days on patrol when cops carried no radios.

"Let me show you something," says Richard Commesso, a retired detective. He pulls out a black-and-white photo of a man with a thick, graying beard. Hard to believe, but it's the clean-shaven Commesso, from his days in a "decoy unit," disguised as a Hasidic Jew to catch a band of Brooklyn muggers.

The stories attest to blue fraternity. But members of the NYC Verrazano 10-13 Association—all retired Staten Island cops—lament today's policing climate, even as they wax about the old days.

"Things have changed drastically," says Commesso, president of the group whose name incorporates the NYPD code for an officer requiring assistance. "If you make an arrest today, there's somebody there with a camera and, my own personal opinion, you're getting a lot of kids today, just out of school, never had a job before, becoming a cop."

Combine officers lacking street savvy and people in minority neighborhoods who mistrust them and policing is much tougher, says Commesso. He credits his long-ago partner, a black cop, with schooling him to the ways of the neighborhoods they patrolled.

"If you go to a high-crime area they have nothing but contempt for you," Hellman says.

The blame belongs to activists who portray cops as enemies rather than allies, says Vincent Montagna, a fellow retired cop.

Members of the NYC Verrazano 10-13 Association, made up of retired police officers, say the Pledge of Allegiance during a meeting in the Staten Island borough of New York, June 15, 2016. (AP Photo/Seth Wenig)

How, exactly, do you build trust between police and people in minority neighborhoods?

On a steamy afternoon, NYPD officers Jessi D'Ambrosio and Mary Gillespie pull up to the Richmond Terrace Houses to start their patrol.

Last year, the city began assigning pairs of officers to specific neighborhoods, rather than having them rush from call to call across precincts. They are mandated to spend a third of their shift "off-radio," talking with residents to forge relationships. The new approach was rolled out to the North Shore in December.

D'Ambrosio, 32, and Gillespie, 28, are the new "neighborhood coordinating officers" for the six-building project where Garner once lived. Jersey Street, with a reputation for crime, runs the length of a complex, most of whose residents are black.

"We want them to feel comfortable with us and that's what we're building on," Gillespie says.

When the two officers, both white and longtime Staten Islanders, walk through the grounds, residents readily return their greetings. During their first hour, they don't answer a single call. Instead, they spend most of it helping Monique Williams, who accidentally locked her two young children inside her car, asleep with the air conditioner running.

Eunice Love, president of the complex's tenants association, recalled years of seeing officers without knowing who they were. But D'Ambrosio and Gillespie? "They're such homeboy, homegirl," Love says. "They know how to get along with people and relate and we love that."

D'Ambrosio measures progress in everyday experience. He and Gillespie give out their cellphone numbers freely. But when one resident called to say she'd spotted a teen wanted for breaking into nearby houses, he took it as a sign of trust. When the pair ticketed cars blocking a wheelchair ramp and an elderly woman thanked them, that was another.

People can resent police after years of negative experiences. Maybe it was being pulled over when they felt they did nothing wrong, or filing a

Police officer Mary Gillespie, left, of the 120th precinct on Staten Island, waves at residents of the Richmond Terrace Houses while on patrol with fellow officer Jessi D'Ambrosio, July 7, 2016. (AP Photo/Mary Altaffer)

noise complaint only to have a cop seemingly brush them off to respond to a more urgent call, D'Ambrosio says.

"It's small steps," he says. "You know you can't just wake up tomorrow and think the world is going to change. But they seem, still, to have accepted us."

Nearly two years after police wrestled Eric Garner to the sidewalk in front of Bay Beauty Supply, his mother, Gwen Carr, stands in the small park across the street and cringes at the scene.

A man who appears to be homeless sprawls across a bench, asleep though it's not yet 1 p.m.

A young woman—"Alcohol Gives You Wings," tattooed down her left arm—sits on the edge of a dry fountain, trying to sell used shoes.

"How much good did they do?" Carr says of police, who arrested her son repeatedly for selling untaxed cigarettes. "Where are they when you need them?"

New York paid $5.9 million to settle claims by Garner's family, including his five children. That does not satisfy Carr. If her son's death means something, officials can clean up this block where regulars, black and white, say drinking and drugs have increased since Garner's death.

Confrontational cops are not the answer, Carr says.

Instead, she wants New York to turn the park into a playground, named for her son. City law reserves playgrounds for children, their parents and guardians. Transforming this triangle would displace the addicts, who could be directed to treatment, and make this area safe, Carr says.

Police should play a role, she says. But too many haven't built relationships with people in the neighborhoods they patrol, Carr says.

"If they did there would be less killing, less crime. The police wouldn't have that much of a problem weeding out the bad guys because the people in the community would let them know," she says. "That is not snitching. That is trying to preserve your community."

That requires trust, though.

"The more I think about it (Garner's death) the madder I get, because that man should not be dead," says Doug Brinson, who sells T-shirts and household items from folding tables on the sidewalk.

Most police are good, but they don't do enough to get rid of the bad ones, says Brinson, who is in his 60s and says he has been arrested for unlawful peddling. Still, he says, the fights, the drinking and the drug use here make clear this neighborhood needs police.

"You've got to have cops on this block," Brinson says, looking down at the makeshift memorial for Garner that he helped build.

"You've got to coexist with the guys on the beat. You've got to. It's only fair."

Logan, West Virginia
To some, Trump is a desperate survival bid

My grandparents fled Appalachia a generation ago. The circumstances they faced in 1967 were similar to what families describe today, 50 years later: Mines were dying, good jobs were hard to find and poverty never lost its grip. Boys were expected to grow up to be coal miners and my grandparents wanted a better life for their sons. So they left Hazard, Kentucky, for a town just outside of Louisville.

I grew up hearing the story of that heart-wrenching decision to leave their home. It was the defining choice of their lives. With that in mind, I asked everyone I talked to for this story the same question: what do you think your town will look like in 10 years? They all gave pretty much the same answer. It'll be a ghost town, or it'll be gone. One man joked that promising kids in Appalachia need to learn the three Rs in school: reading, writing and a roadmap to Charlotte.

We decided to go to West Virginia to see what political choice means to people left behind by American progress. This is a place full of people who have lost all hope that their children might have a future here. Their friends and neighbors are fleeing; their towns are hollowing out. They believe in roots and family and loyalty, but they also believe that unless something drastic changes they will have no choice but to leave this place behind too.

My dad often talks of how grateful he is that his parents made that hard choice to leave so that he _ and I _ might have a better future. But my grandmother still misses the mountains she left behind.

—Claire Galofaro, AP Correspondent

* * *

Mike Kirk leans across the counter of the pawnshop where he works for $11 an hour. It's less than half what he made in the mines, but the best he can do these days.

He and two customers ponder what this city might look like in 10 years if nothing changes. Many of the storefronts on the narrow downtown streets are empty. Some of the buildings burned. Their blackened shells, "condemned" signs taped to the doors, stand as a symbol of how far they've fallen.

In 10 years? A ghost town, one customer offers. The other wonders if it might simply cease to exist.

There are places like this across America—poor and getting poorer, feeling left behind while the rest got richer. But nowhere has the plummet of the white working class been as merciless as here in central Appalachia. And nowhere have the cross-currents of desperation and boiling resentment that have devoured a presidential race been on such glaring display.

It used to be that young people could finish high school and get a job in the mines that paid enough to feed their families. Now the mines are idle. The railroad tracks that used to back up traffic as coal trains barreled through town sit mostly silent, weeds growing up around the ties.

Families are fleeing. The population of Logan County is 35,000, half what it was 50 years ago. More than 96 percent of residents are white; one in five lives in poverty; few have college degrees. Drug abuse is rampant. The life expectancy for men is 68 years old; they die eight years younger than the average American man.

Even cremations are up at the funeral home down the street. People can't afford caskets anymore.

"Look around, this town went to hell," said Kirk, who lost his $28-an-hour job on a strip mine and his three-bedroom house with a two-car garage. He and his wife and children moved in with his mother. He took this pawn shop job because it paid a little more than the used car dealership, his only other option. His town has grown full of for-sale signs as family after family says goodbye and moves to one of those places that fared far better as Appalachia fell apart.

The unemployment rate is 11 percent, compared to less than 5 percent nationwide. Many have given up working altogether: West Virginia is the only state in America where less than half of working-aged people work.

Former mine worker turned pawn shop employee, Mike Kirk, talks with customers in Logan, W.VA, May 11, 2016. (AP Photo/Claire Galofaro)

More than 12 percent of Logan County residents collect Social Security disability checks, three times the national average.

They gave up on their politicians—they elected both Republicans and Democrats and believe both failed them in favor of chasing campaign contributions from the class above them and votes from the one below, the neighbors they suspect would rather collect government welfare than get a job.

Anxiety turned to despair, said James Branscome, a retired managing director of Standard & Poor's and a former staff member at the Appalachian Regional Commission. And desperate people, throughout history, have turned to tough-talking populists.

And that is how, in one of America's forgotten corners, the road was perfectly paved for the ascent of Donald Trump. He won by spectacular margins all across the coalfields. From Appalachia to the Rust Belt to the hollowing manufacturing towns in the Midwest, Trump collected his most ardent supporters in places like this.

"He offers us hope," Kirk said, "and hope's the one thing we have left."

Peter Atwater, a consultant who studies the tides of consumer confidence, describes the collapse of the coalfields as a microcosm of the indignation burning across America that has come to define the 2016 campaign. Its power may determine the next president of the United States.

The average Republican is as pessimistic about the economy today as the day Lehman Brothers collapsed, eight years ago, Atwater said. That perception of decline—that the country is careening in the wrong direction—can be as politically potent as watching your hometown wither, he said.

The non-profit Public Religion Research Institute calls such people "nostalgia voters." Daniel Cox, the organization's research director, said an uneven recovery from the recession lined up with societal shifts—the election of the first non-white president, a rising minority population, the decreasing influence of Christian values. It left many in struggling, blue-collar communities across the country feeling deserted for the sake of progress someplace else.

"Today, we're not interested in the plan, we're interested in the slogan," Atwater said. "When confidence falls, it's all too complicated to

Shuttered storefronts in downtown Logan, W.VA. (AP Photo/Claire Galofaro)

understand an elaborate plan or an articulated policy. We don't want to wait for the details; we don't want to read the footnotes. Just give me a powerful headline."

Trump promised to build the wall. Create jobs. Destroy ISIS. He blamed immigrants and China and Muslims for America's woes.

He stood on a stage in West Virginia, put on a hard hat and panto-mimed shoveling coal. He promised to make them win again.

His critics warn that his red-blooded, racially tinged rants threaten to unravel the very fabric of the nation. Here, the same words translate as truth-telling.

His call caught fire so fervently that some are staking their families' futures on whether he wins in November.

Like Ashley Kominar, a 33-year-old mother of three whose husband lost his job in the mines in Mingo County. She now knows what it means to choose whether to buy food or pay the electric bill.

Kominar is a registered Democrat, like almost everybody else here. This region was reliably Democratic for generations. Then the once-mighty United Mine Workers of America crumbled in the 1990s, and Democrats lost their grip. Last month, in a place where President Bill Clinton had been greeted like a rock star, Hillary Clinton was heckled and flipped the bird.

Kominar considers Trump a businessman: tough, a little too combative, but so different from any politician she's seen that he just might be able to save this place. If he wins, she will stay in West Virginia. If he loses, she said, she will flee.

"I don't know exactly what's in his head, what his vision is for us," she said. "But I know he has one and that's what counts."

The phone in Truman Chafin's office in Mingo County rang three times before noon on a recent Thursday, and each time the friend on the line detailed their economic plight: lost jobs, missed mortgage payments, hungry children.

Chafin, a Democrat who represented this district in the state Senate for 32 years before voters ousted him in a Republican sweep of the statehouse in 2014, mocks Trump and his promise to fix it all; he even dressed up like him for a Halloween party. But he understands the drumbeat of disappointment that has led so many of his neighbors to plunk signs in their yards that read "Make America Great Again."

"They're looking for somebody to give them some hope and here comes this elixir salesman who says, 'Drink this and all will be good,'" Chafin said. "He's playing to the short-term sound bites and that's what people want to hear."

Chafin's own daughter relocated to South Carolina and told him she'll never move back. There's nothing left for her here, she told him.

There are pockets like this across America. A think tank called the Economic Innovation Group created the Distressed Communities Index, which combines several factors for every county—poverty rate, the percentage of people without a college degree, the number of abandoned homes.

The most distressed patches stretch through Appalachia and across the deep South, cutting across swing states like North Carolina, Ohio, Virginia and Florida. Trump won in rich places and poor places and places in between. But an analysis shows that Trump's strongest support among early primary Republican voters increased along with the level of economic hardship in their communities.

In Hamilton County, Florida, 29 percent of the population lives in poverty, two-thirds of adults don't work and the median household income stands at $35,629, nearly $20,000 less than the American average. Trump collected 57 percent of the primary vote. In Columbus County, North Carolina, which suffers similar statistics, Trump won 61 percent.

Buchanan County, Virginia, is much like its West Virginia neighbors. The unemployment rate hovers higher than 10 percent. Young people are fleeing in droves. A quarter of people live in poverty and one in five rely on disability. In March, 70 percent of primary voters cast their ballot for Trump, with four other candidates still in the race.

"Americans are becoming fed up with politicians promising them the moon and delivering them far less," said Gerald Arrington, Buchanan County's elected county prosecutor, a 37-year-old Democrat who cast his first ballot for Bill Clinton in 1996. This time he voted for Trump.

"Everyone is so used to politician-speak. He's refreshing," he said. "Maybe part of it is his ego. His ego is going to make him want to be the greatest president ever. He's a winner."

After a recent Trump rally in West Virginia, countless news articles and academics dismissed Trump's pledge to bring back coal as impossible, tied to market forces and geology. Chuck Keeney, a professor of political science and history at Southern Community College in Logan, often hears his students dismiss the criticism as the establishment, the very machine that ignored them for so long, beating up on Trump now, too.

"What they see in their minds is the elite that looks down on them, mocks them, makes fun of them, thinks they're stupid," Keeney said. "They see all those establishment groups ganging up on Donald Trump and that makes them root for him more."

Albert Adams worked at a mine for 27 years until every day started to bring more bad news. Layoffs. Slashed hours. Cut pay. He and a friend saved their money for a year, quit their jobs and opened up Big Al's Auto and Small Engine Repair to try to build a life after coal.

They hung a "Make America Great Again" sign over the coffee maker.

* * *

Albert Adams and Leslie Arthur, owners of Big Al's Auto and Small Engine Repair, sit in their offices in Logan, W.VA. They quit their jobs in the mines when they figured the coal industry wouldn't bounce back. (AP Photo/Claire Galofaro)

Adams doesn't like everything Trump has to say, particularly about immigration. He imagines immigrants are a lot like West Virginians: hard workers, doomed by the place of their birth to be down on their luck, looking for a better life.

His conundrum is echoed all over these mountains. People like Trump's delivery, the rat-a-tat-tat of promises and insults so unscripted they figure he couldn't have given it enough forethought to be pandering. Yet they're occasionally disturbed by the contents.

Adams' business partner, Leslie Arthur, isn't quite sure Trump should be trusted with the nuclear codes. Mike Honaker, who runs the local funeral home, doesn't appreciate how he talks about women. Mike Kirk in the pawn shop cringes when he hurls schoolyard taunts.

But they agree with him more often than not and they're willing to forgive because they believe the political machine left them with no other option.

Coalfield communities have always been poor. But life here has never felt this hopeless, Adams said. People can no longer imagine what a future might look like. Coal will never completely bounce back. There are no factories, no infrastructure to build any and no companies that want to relocate to a place cut off from the rest of America by mountains.

So piles of lawnmowers and weed-eaters grow outside Adams' new shop. People he's known his whole life come by often trying to sell whatever they have left to pay their rent, keep their cars running, feed their kids.

"If this town does come back, I'll be dead and gone before we see it," Adams said.

He and Arthur hammered a new wheel onto a Ford, a $300 job they did on credit because the out-of-work miner can't afford it right now.

They knew opening this shop was a gamble. Maybe they'll win and stay afloat, maybe they won't. Maybe Trump can fix it. Maybe it can't be fixed.

Adams doesn't fault his friends and neighbors who left it behind.

Sometimes he thinks of packing it all up and moving himself. He figures he'd head west, where the coal seams still run thick.

Atlanta
Clinton highlights lack of women in office

When we first decided to examine the number of women in elected office, I expected to find a lack of parity but I was surprised at the extent that women were underrepresented across all levels of government. Although women represent more than half of the population, they account for just a fifth of all U.S. representatives and senators and one in four state lawmakers. Of the nation's 50 governors, only six are women. They serve as mayors in roughly 19 percent of the nation's largest cities.

In totality, the numbers were striking. It was also interesting to discover that women had made huge gains during the 1980s and early 1990s, but progress had largely stalled in the years since. Experts had various reasons for that, but what struck me was that research has shown that, when they run, women win as often as men do. The problem is simply a lack of women running for office. So that led me to those women who are out there knocking on doors and asking for votes so I could learn more about what inspires them.

What I heard from almost every woman I interviewed was a commitment to helping other women run for office as well. They credited their mentors with giving them the encouragement to run and, perhaps more importantly, showing them that it was OK to want to do this. It was surprising to hear that, even in 2016, female candidates are still asked about who will take care of their children if they are elected. As one candidate noted, voters were unlikely to ask that of her male opponent.

One woman I interviewed, who didn't end up in the story because we had so many great examples, told me about how she often brings her 6-year-old son with her when she campaigns so he can see the value of public service. I suspect he is also learning another important lesson, that women can love their families, be good parents and be successful in whatever career they choose.

— Christina A. Cassidy, AP State Government Reporter

* * *

Hillary Clinton and Mary Thomas have little in common, except for this: They both hope to add to the meager ranks of America's female elected officials come January.

You know about Clinton, but probably not Thomas—a conservative Republican, opponent of abortion and Obamacare, former general counsel of Florida's Department of Elder Affairs. She's running in Florida's 2nd District to become the first Indian-American woman in Congress. It's no easy task.

"There is still a good ol' boys network that is in place," she says, though she insists that "A lot of people see the value in having different types of people in Washington."

Even as Clinton attempts to shatter what she has called "the highest, hardest glass ceiling," other women like Thomas are testing other, lower ceilings. There are many: Women in the U.S. remain significantly underrepresented at all levels of elected office.

"Historically, we have centuries of catching up to do," says Missy Shorey, executive director of the conservative-leaning Maggie's List, one of a number of groups supporting female candidates.

Republican candidate for Florida's Second Congressional District Mary Thomas, right, talks to supporters at DSH Firearms in Tallahassee, FL, July 19, 2016. (AP Photo/Mark Wallheiser)

Though women are more than half of the American population, they now account for just a fifth of all U.S. representatives and senators, and one in four state lawmakers. They serve as governors of only six states and are mayors in roughly 19 percent of the nation's largest cities.

There has been progress; as recently as 1978, there were no women U.S. senators, and now there are 20. Still, there has been little headway since a surge of women won office in the 1980s and early 1990s. Sixteen states have fewer women serving in legislatures than in 2005, and five others have shown no improvement, according to an analysis by The Associated Press of data collected by the National Conference of State Legislatures.

It is another aspect of the gender divide—one of the most glaring in our society. Women still earn 79 cents for every dollar men take home; men outnumber women in higher paying occupations, though even there they are often paid less. And the division plays out politically, as well. Women have tended to vote with the Democrats more often; polls have shown

Clinton with a double-digit lead over Donald Trump among women, and Trump leading Clinton by double digits among men.

Advocates say the dearth of women officeholders has had consequences. They say women's voices have been muted in local, state and national discussions of all issues, from climate change to foreign policy, but particularly of concerns important to women and working mothers: family leave, child care and equal pay, for example. They point to instances where women in office have made a difference.

Kim McMillan was first elected as a Democrat to her seat in Tennessee's House of Representatives in 1994 when she was 32 years old, a working mother of two children under the age of 3. She was motivated to run after visiting the state Capitol as part of her law practice.

Kim McMillan, D-Clarksville, was first elected in 1994 when she was 32 and a working mother of two children under age 3. She was motivated to run after visiting the state Capitol. "There were no women that I could see," she said. (AP Photo/Mark Humphrey)

"I went up to the gallery upstairs and you could look out at the entire House of Representatives. I remember standing up there and looking at the House floor, and I didn't see anybody who looked like me," McMillan says. "There were no women that I could see."

More than once, she was told she couldn't win because she was a woman. She recalls being asked why she would run with two young children to care for.

McMillan won that race and eventually served six terms, rising to become the first woman majority leader. A major accomplishment: expansion of pre-kindergarten education around the state.

"I felt like I represented people who didn't have any representation, working mothers like me," says McMillan, who now serves as the first female mayor of Clarksville, the fifth largest city in Tennessee.

Whether a Clinton win in November will inspire a new generation of female politicians remains to be seen. While the election of a woman as U.S. president would be unprecedented, at least 52 other countries around the world have had a female head of state in the last 50 years. Great Britain got its second female prime minister when Theresa May took office this month.

Female representation varies significantly around the U.S. Six states have never elected or appointed a woman to the U.S. House of Representatives, and 22 have never had a woman represent them in the U.S. Senate. Mississippi is the only state where a woman has never served as a congresswoman, U.S. senator or governor.

Colorado has the highest number of women serving in a state legislature, with 42 percent, but it has never had a woman governor or U.S. senator.

And while Nikki Haley is South Carolina's governor, the state has never sent a woman to the U.S. Senate and has one of the lowest percentages of female state lawmakers at 14 percent.

A major problem, activists say, is convincing women to run. Researchers say women generally need to be recruited to seek elected office, whereas men are more likely to decide on their own. Men are also the ones who are more likely to be recruited.

"We know that when women run for office, they win as often as men do," says Debbie Walsh, executive director of the Center for American Women and Politics at Rutgers University. "The number of women running isn't going up, and so the number of women in office isn't going up."

Quotas have been credited by some researchers with boosting the number of women in office in a few countries, but the political parties in the U.S. are unlikely to consider any such system. Instead, the work of recruiting and supporting women has largely fallen to outside groups such as EMILY's List.

Founded in 1985, the group backs Democrats who support abortion rights. It points to a record of helping elect 19 women to the U.S. Senate, 110 women to the U.S. House of Representatives and more than 700 women to state and local offices, including 11 governors.

It's not just financial support, although EMILY's List says it has raised more than $400 million since it was created. The group works to recruit female candidates, offering them training and guidance in such areas as hiring staff, developing a financial plan and honing campaign messages. It also offers a support network of elected officials who can mentor female candidates.

"No matter who you are, when running for office for the first time you have a lot of questions and need answers," says Marcy Stech, who oversees communications for EMILY's List. "We want to help them make sure those boxes are checked."

A support network has been instrumental throughout Ellen Rosenblum's career, beginning as a lawyer in Oregon and continuing as she was appointed a state court judge and later during her successful bid for state attorney general. Two of her early mentors were former Oregon Supreme Court Justice Betty Roberts, the first woman to serve on an Oregon appellate court, and Barbara Roberts, the first woman elected governor of Oregon.

Rosenblum says she worked to pay it forward, helping to build up a statewide group of women lawyers. When it came to deciding in late 2011 whether to launch her first bid for statewide office, that same network was instrumental.

"I needed lots and lots of advice," says Rosenblum, who at the time had just retired as a judge. "I needed women to talk to, to make sure I was not completely out of my mind to do this."

The first woman elected as Oregon's attorney general, Rosenblum is seeking a second term in November.

Oregon Attorney General Ellen Rosenblum at her office in Portland, OR, July 13, 2016. (AP Photo/Don Ryan)

In California, Hannah-Beth Jackson had long been active in her community beyond her work as a lawyer and former prosecutor, but it took the encouragement of one of her mentors to convince her to run for state Assembly in 1998.

"Women tend to ask permission, and we're never quite sure we are good enough or ready enough," she says. "Men generally don't have those same concerns."

Now in the state Senate, she is chairwoman of the powerful judiciary committee as well as the California Legislative Women's Caucus. Jackson's legislative accomplishments include what was considered the strongest equal pay legislation in the country.

Despite her influence and tenure, the Democratic lawmaker does not always succeed. Earlier this year, a bill she sponsored extending California's family leave protections to small-business employees died in an all-male committee amid concerns of regulatory burdens.

She is undeterred.

"Let's see what happens when I bring the bill back," Jackson says. "Hopefully, that committee will have some women members."

....

Seattle, WA
Gender equality? It's complicated

by David Crary, AP National Social Issues Reporter

For weeks after the vote, the abuse kept coming: Venomous, sexist phone calls and emails, venting rage at the five women on Seattle's City Council who outvoted four men to derail a sports arena project.

"Disgraceful hag" was one of the milder messages. "Go home and climb in the oven," one councilor was told.

This unfolded not in 1966, during an era when American women mobilized en masse to demand equality, but 50 years later in May of 2016 — two months before the first woman was nominated to lead a major party's presidential ticket.

It's a complicated time for gender relations in the U.S., as the campaign pitting Hillary Clinton against Donald Trump has underscored — most recently, with the fallout from their first debate and a sharp exchange about Trump's attention to a former Miss Universe and her weight.

On one hand there's been great progress toward equality. Women have climbed to the top of many a corporate ladder, IBM and General Motors being just two examples. They were recently approved to serve in all military combat jobs, and depending on the election outcome, troops could soon be saluting the first female commander in chief.

At the same time, deep and obvious gaps remain — not only in terms of economic inequality and continuing discrimination and harassment in the workplace, but in everyday actions and conversations.

Consider this year's reboot of "Ghostbusters," with women replacing the male leads of the original. Misogynistic comments circulated on social media demanding the film's stars appear nude or be "hot."

Or the way some sports commentators covered women's accomplishments at the Rio Olympics. An NBC newsman drew criticism for referencing the husband-coach of a Hungarian swimmer as the "guy responsible" for her record-breaking performance.

Or the backlash in, of all places, progressive Seattle, after the five female councilors voted against the proposed sale of a street to help make way for a new arena that could host an NBA team.

One local attorney, in a signed email to all five women, described them as "disgraceful pieces of trash" and added, "I can only hope that you each find ways to quickly and painfully end yourselves." He later apologized.

Council member Lorena Gonzalez, a lawyer whose past work included representing victims of sexual abuse and harassment, said the Seattle controversy "hit a nerve" because it coincided with a presidential campaign that has exacerbated gender tensions. Women of all political persuasions needed to band together to "push back" against such treatment, she said.

Just a few decades ago, women rarely held the collective political power that they now wield in Seattle. In many male-dominated domains, women's strides have been slow-paced and, even then, often greeted with resentment.

"Cultural change often comes with some backlash," said Emily Martin, the National Women's Law Center's general counsel. "Some people feel threatened by women's progress. Making vile attacks on the internet is an easy way to express yourself if the world is changing in ways you feel are threatening."

That culture clash has become striking in this election year. As feminists celebrated Clinton's glass-shattering nomination with the slogan "I'm With Her," Trump said the only thing Clinton had going for her was "the woman's card." Some of his supporters wear "Trump that Bitch" T-shirts.

In the opening debate, after Trump questioned her looks and stamina, Clinton quickly pivoted to the issue of sexism.

"This is a man who called women pigs, slobs and dogs," she said.

Polls show Clinton, a Democrat, benefiting from a gender gap that's been a fact of American politics since 1980, with women voting for her party more reliably than men in each presidential election. This year's gap could be the biggest ever; a New York Times poll in mid-September showed Trump, a Republican, leading among likely male voters by 11 percentage points, while Clinton led among likely female voters by 13 points

There's also a gender gap in turnout—nearly 10 million more women voted than men in 2012.

Brooke Ackerly, a political science professor at Vanderbilt who specializes in gender issues, said the sexist sentiments on display during the campaign aren't new to American politics, but are louder and more visible than
before.

"It suggests to me there's some latent anger that's being given permission to express itself," said Ackerly, adding that Trump was the catalyst for
this. "What's new is that we're seeing it in public."

Clinton, of course, has long been targeted by sexist taunts, and says
she's learned to take them in stride.

Still, said Debbie Walsh, director of the Center for American Women
and Politics at Rutgers University, "I'm concerned about what it means for
younger women who see this as what you might confront if you dare to tread
on what is seen as male turf."

As a profession, elective politics remains predominantly male turf.
Women comprise more than half the U.S. population, yet account for just
a fifth of all members of Congress and one-fourth of state lawmakers,
according to an Associated Press survey earlier this year. And that's a better
showing than for women in such fields as firefighting, construction and video-game design.

For two years, software engineer Brianna Wu of Boston has been a target of the online harassment campaign known as Gamergate, which sub-
jected several women in the video-game industry to misogynistic threats. It
surfaced in the summer of 2014, and hasn't vanished.

"It's still a constant drumbeat," said Wu, who became a target after ridiculing those who decried women's advances in the male-dominated industry. Pictures of her previous house were posted online by harassers. She
and her husband now use a re-mailing service to get packages, and resort to
pseudonyms when they must provide their real address.

"It's exhausting," she said. "It's just a cost of your career, if you're a
woman."

Depending on the questions posed, opinion polls show curiously mixed
views on gender issues. For example, polling by Gallup shows that 92 percent of Americans—including overwhelming majorities of both men and
women—would vote for a woman for president if they felt she was qualified.

Yet there's a split as to whether obstacles remain that make it harder
for women to get ahead. About 63 percent of women say this is the case,

compared to 41 percent of men, according to a recent Pew Research Center survey.

Among white men, Trump's strongest base of support, there's some cynicism about the whole gender debate.

"We're so sick of the gender card being played, we don't even listen to it," said Mark Meckler, a Trump backer and co-founder of the Tea Party Patriots who lives near Sacramento, California.

Throughout her campaign, Clinton has presented herself as a champion of women's issues, promising to protect their rights to abortion and fight to reduce economic inequalities.

Trump has recently stepped up appeals directed at women. He advocated making birth control available without a prescription and offered proposals on child care and paid parental leave.

Critics said his child-care plan, by relying on a tax deduction rather than a credit, would skew to the advantage of wealthier families. As for parental leave, Clinton advocates coverage for fathers and mothers. Trump's proposal covers only mothers; some advocacy groups say this would make companies less likely to hire women since they could lose them for six weeks in the event of childbirth.

Pay equity is another issue with gender overtones; surveys show that nearly two-thirds of minimum wage earners are women.

Clinton says she supports raising the federal minimum wage from $7.25 to $12 an hour. Trump said in July that the minimum wage should be $10, but added that states should "really call the shots."

In some places, there are efforts to address the gender wage gap locally. A ballot measure in Cincinnati calls for a new tax levy to expand access to preschool education, and one of its goals is to boost pay for preschool workers, many of them women of color earning wages that barely support their families. In Ohio, preschool teachers earned an average of $23,690 a year in 2014.

Among the organizers working for the measure is Elizabeth Hopkins, 31, an African-American mother of children aged 1 and 3.

"It saddens me, that the jobs these women have keep them in poverty," Hopkins said. "These are the most important positions. They're the ones tending to our children."

Trump/Clinton differences are particularly stark on abortion. Clinton favors lifting a ban on use of federal funds to help poor women afford abortions; Trump says he would appoint "pro-life" Supreme Court justices who might consider overturning the Roe v. Wade ruling that established a nationwide right to abortion.

Unsurprisingly, Clinton is backed by the National Organization for Women and Planned Parenthood. Trump's supporters include leaders of national anti-abortion groups.

Some prospective voters don't fit easily into the obvious boxes. There are conservative women who would never vote for Clinton, yet find Trump's rhetoric and behavior repugnant. There are men planning to vote for Clinton who wish she would be as outspoken about challenges facing boys and fathers as those facing women and girls.

One of those men is author Warren Farrell of Mill Valley, California, a figure in what's loosely known as "the men's movement."

"I'm supporting Hillary Clinton despite the people in her campaign who are less compassionate toward men, less understanding of the importance of fathers and almost completely ignorant of the boy crisis," said Farrell. That's a reference to boys' worse grades in school and higher rates of learning disabilities, disciplinary problems and dropout rates than girls.

As for Trump, "he represents everything that women fear about men — blustery, grandiose, narcissistic," Farrell said.

Meanwhile, Trump has many enthusiastic female supporters, including Amber Smith, who served in Iraq and Afghanistan as a helicopter pilot with the Army's 101st Airborne Division.

"I like that he has a backbone and he's not politically correct," she said.

Now a writer and commentator with a just-published memoir, Smith perceives Clinton as seeking to portray women as victims.

"We live in a country that provides equal opportunities for men and woman," Smith said. "I'm an example of that. I wanted to be an air mission commander based on my own merits and skill level, not because of my gender."

South Boston, Virginia
Even in fractured land, there's much unity

The first thing that hits you at Annin Flagmakers is the smell, the air thick with glue and ink. Then, as you weave your way through the cavernous warehouse, the noise grows stronger, a relentless din of jackhammering needles. And, finally, it's the sensory blast you've waited for, the sewing room awash in stars and stripes from wall to sprawling wall, and miles of red, white and blue.

I went to this factory near the Virginia-North Carolina border because there's no more potent symbol of American patriotism than our flag, and it seemed one of the few things that largely unite us. But Annin's workers made clear there is more. Regardless of their political leanings, they repeated similar values, of faith and family and hard work. Those things, they said, were the meaning of their handi-work, of the millions of flags that roll off their production line.

The factory's director of operations, Gary Gibson, leads me through the endless racks of inventory, for countries from Turkmenistan to Monaco to Palau. The American flag is the heart of their business and, while it evokes varying emotions in people, Gibson says his workers all feel a sense of pride in what they create.

It's a big and diverse country and it's easy to overthink what defines us. My trip to Annin affirmed the simple things that link neighbor to neighbor, coast to coast. It's a season of vilification and nastiness and labels, but the good people of Annin remind us what's easy to forget: How much we all share.

—Matt Sedensky, National Writer

* * *

Outside the Annin Flagmakers factory in this perennial swing state, a summer of discontent is brewing. They feel the country's divides inside, too—gulfs between rich and poor, left and right, this side and that side, that seem to grow deeper with each passing week.

Yet as their hands glide over broad red and white stripes and sew bright stars to blue rectangles, crafting the most unifying American symbol, the flagmakers sound far more alike than different.

Asked to name life's most important elements, the same answers come back: family, work and faith. Presented with the idea of living in a foreign land, they uniformly say no, America can't be beat. Nudged to sum up the values Americans broadly share, they point to their handiwork and what it stands for—freedom, opportunity and pride.

"We may be divided on some things, but when it comes down to the most important things we come together," said Emily Bouldin, a 66-year-old seated before a jabbering sewing machine on an Annin production floor awash in red, white and blue. "Because we realize, together we stand, divided we fall."

The splintering that is bared in the overheated rhetoric of a presidential campaign only tells so much. Survey data, the work of academics studying the national ethos and conversations with individuals across the country make clear another truth: Americans are remarkably united, too.

You see it in the banality of routine, in morning drives to work and evenings before the glow of a TV; in lines to buy Powerball tickets and in

An employee works on the fringe of a U.S. flag at Annin Flagmakers in South Boston, VA, July 6, 2016. (AP Photo/Gerry Broome)

proud parents amassed on Little League diamonds. You see it along parade routes, in blood donation lines after tragedies, and in the quiet prayers of the faithful. You see it in the flag.

"The United States is the freest and the best country on this earth and that flag represents that," said Ed Haney, a 69-year-old maintenance mechanic at the Annin plant. "The country was founded by men of different opinions who united on one thing: The freedom to have those opinions."

Haney and Bouldin work on opposite ends of the sprawling sewing room floor, and political pollsters would see them in different worlds altogether. Haney is white and male, tends to side with Republicans and expects to give his vote to Donald Trump in the fall. Bouldin is black and female, always votes Democratic and plans to cast her ballot for Hillary Clinton. Yet they both speak of their Christian faith, the importance of family, their love of America and what the flag represents.

"It really is the land of the free," Bouldin said.

American agreement is harder to gauge than division, observes Tom Smith, director of an eminent yardstick of public opinion, the General Social Survey at the University of Chicago. "By their very nature, surveys don't go out and ask people about things that there's near unanimity about," he says, "because that's rarely interesting." Still, he notes data captures glimpses of consensus on a range of topics across the U.S. as well as points of national pride and clues on the ways Americans think and live.

Surveys find nearly all Americans believe in helping the less fortunate, in entrepreneurism and small business, and in public schools.

On foreign affairs, they hold resoundingly favorable views of Canada, Great Britain, France, Germany and Japan, and unfavorable ones of North Korea, Iran, Iraq and Afghanistan. Overwhelmingly, they see the Islamic State group as a major threat.

Most Americans expect the U.S. to fight in another war in the coming years.

Domestically, there's near unanimity that veterans should be better cared for, and that more research into renewable energy should be supported. Medicare and Social Security are wildly popular across age groups. The federal budget should be balanced, a big majority agrees.

Patrick Miller, a political science professor at the University of Kansas who studies partisanship and polling, said Americans unite around national pride, symbols such as the flag and pop culture. And though the public is moving closer to mirroring the fierce polarization of politicians, he said, people remain close on many issues.

"The average Democrat and the average Republican are not that far apart from each other," Miller said.

To those who insist today marks the country's most divided time, political scientist David O'Connell says look to history: Early political rivalries were sometimes resolved with duels. The United States was disunited by years of Civil War. Andrew Jackson openly spoke of hanging his vice president.

It's true that political party differences have sharpened lately—conservative Democrats and liberal Republicans are near extinction, and many legislators don't dare work across the aisle—but average Americans aren't nearly as divided as their lawmakers.

"The people attending the Democratic and Republican conventions this summer do have more extreme opinions than in the past," said O'Connell, a political science professor at Dickinson College in Carlisle, Pennsylvania. "But the public? The public remains moderate and open to compromise."

Even on topics considered among the most contentious, unity can sometimes be found.

The gun debate may polarize Capitol Hill and statehouses, but there is wide consensus among Americans on mandating background checks for gun shows and private sales (85 percent agree, according to a Pew Research Center poll), and on keeping weapons from the mentally ill (79 percent agree).

Though abortion remains acrimonious, comparatively few people call for totally legalizing or outlawing it in every case, with the majority of people somewhere in the middle. (Only 24 percent of Americans believe in blanket legalization, according to Pew, and 16 percent are for an outright ban.)

And though immigration remains a flashpoint, including the idea of building a wall along the U.S.-Mexico border, most Americans believe undocumented immigrants should be able to remain in the country if they meet certain conditions. (Another Pew poll found 74 percent of Americans held that view.)

Sewing machine operators assemble U.S. flags at Annin Flagmakers, which has seen the ebbs and flows of American patriotism. After 9/11, business was 20 times the norm. (AP Photo/Gerry Broome)

A sense of American unity also begins to emerge when comparing the U.S. with other countries, especially in the developed world. Public opinion polls show Americans, far more than those elsewhere, believe hard work is very important to get ahead in life and that individuals have control over their success in life. Americans also express a sense of hope and optimism that's rare among wealthy countries: They are far more likely, according to Pew, to describe their day as a particularly good one.

Strikingly, Americans stand out among rich countries for their widespread belief in God, the importance of religion in their lives and the regularity in which they practice their faith. Some 89 percent of Americans express some level of belief in God, according to Pew.

It is not just the weightier facets of life that unify the nation.

Americans love to eat out so much that spending on restaurants and bars—an estimated $54 billion in June, according to the U.S. Department of Commerce—has eclipsed that in grocery stores. Wherever they dine, they love red meat and ice cream and cheese, USDA data shows.

They love shopping. They spend more than five hours a week in stores, according to the American Time Use Survey.

And they love dogs. An Associated Press survey reaching that unsurprising conclusion also noted cats get far more mixed reviews.

Sports bring Americans together, even though team rivalries thrive. Chants of "USA" resound as Olympians compete. The Super Bowl is so popular it has become a de facto national holiday, with more than one-third of the country tuning in to the game. Countless hours are spent fielding fantasy teams or filling in office March Madness brackets.

Many of these everyday markers of consensus were on display on a sun-drenched July day on the National Mall in Washington, where people jogged in team T-shirts, walked their dogs or grabbed lunch at a food truck—all on a stretch showcasing grand-scale symbols of American unity.

Darlene and Tom Stetson rested between two of the Lincoln Memorial's towering pillars and pondered the question of what unifies the country.

"Sports" was the first thought of Darlene Stetson, a 62-year-old third-grade teacher. Diverse communities come together to cheer their common team.

Her husband, a 61-year-old who works in finance, offered, "Family, school and work."

The couple, who had traveled from their home in Louisville, Kentucky, acknowledged America's problems and divisions.

But, he said, "I still think this is the greatest country."

She agreed: "Whenever I've been out of the country, I can't wait to come home."

Such feelings are pervasive. A poll from The Associated Press-NORC Center for Public Affairs Research found a large majority of Americans regard the U.S. as one of the greatest countries, even as that survey also affirmed deep splits on politics today.

Americans even find agreement on their weaknesses. Surveys show most lack much confidence in Congress or the overall political system, most doubt Clinton or Trump will unify the country, and more than eight in 10 people believe the country is more divided than in the past.

In the AP-NORC poll, when asked to describe the U.S. in one word, respondents' answers diverged sharply: Though "freedom" and "great" were the most-uttered responses, words like "struggling," "declining" and their synonyms, taken together, made up the greatest fraction of answers.

One poll respondent, Alleen Anderson, an 89-year-old retired cattle rancher in Red Oak, Texas, described the country as awesome, said she believed the nation's best days are ahead and that the U.S. will be less divided in the future.

"I still believe that people will look at one another, find the good parts of each other and the country will be better," said Anderson, who expects to vote for Trump.

Nearly a thousand miles away, on the edge of Lake Michigan, 25-year-old Qymana Botts comes from a different generation and a different mindset than Anderson. She lives in Gary, Indiana, is working on a master's degree in education and describes herself as a liberal who will vote for Dr. Jill Stein if the Green Party candidate makes it on her state's ballot. In one word, she describes America as frustrating, but she doesn't see it as more divided than the past and believes its best days are ahead.

Botts sees most Americans' desires as the same: stability for their families and to have a good job. She thinks people are more inclusive toward those of different backgrounds than they once were and more aware of

Maintenance technician Buddy Wilborn works on a sewing machine at Annin Flagmakers in South Boston, VA. He's not so sure who he'll vote for come November and knows the election could drive a wedge. But he sees hope. "I think our country is starting to come back together," he said. (AP Photo/Gerry Broome)

different viewpoints. America is still great, she said, and she wouldn't want to live anywhere else.

"We actually, as a society, agree on the most important stuff," Botts said.

That unity is embodied in the flag. American children start their school days, hand to heart, in a pledge to the flag, and it becomes as much a fixture in their lives as in their history books. It was raised on Iwo Jima and has been draped over Olympians, launched into space and planted at the North Pole. After 9/11, it was flown atop the wreckage of the World Trade Center, pinned to lapels and added to front porches from sea to sea.

Annin Flagmakers has seen the ebbs and flows of American patriotism. It opened in 1847 and saw its first sales spike after the Civil War inspired unity across the North. Demand boomed again with World Wars I and II. During the Vietnam War, when fervent opposition led some to burn flags in protest, business was lean, but bicentennial celebrations in 1976 brought a new surge of orders. After 9/11, business was 20 times the norm.

It's just past Independence Day at the company's cavernous factory near the Virginia-North Carolina line. It is thick with the smell of dye and glue and the din of jackhammering needles. There is a boom in business now, too, and the plant added a third shift to accommodate demand.

The company isn't entirely sure what's driving the orders. Maybe it's the heated presidential election or the drumbeat of tragedies. Buddy Wilborn, a 59-year-old taking a break from repairing sewing machines, isn't so sure either. But he sees some signs American unity is remerging.

When there are trying times, whether terrorism or natural disaster or a hardball political season that drives wedges between people, he sees the flag's resonance grow. He's not so sure who he'll vote for come November, but he sees hope.

"I think our country is starting to come back together," he said.

....

From Sea to Shining Sea
America in one word?

by Matt Sedensky, National Writer

Free and great, or divided and confused. Diverse and powerful, or troubled and broken. In search of a single word encapsulating their country at this moment, Americans offered pollsters a lexicon reflecting both hope and dissonance.

The most-uttered word from about 1,000 responses to the Associated Press-NORC Center for Public Affairs Research survey was "freedom," with "free" not far behind at No. 4. "Great" took second place — and "good," "powerful," "wonderful" and "awesome" also occupied the top tier. But crowding the list were entries mirroring national angst.

"Divided" ranked third, and "confused" and "troubled" tied for fifth, amassed alongside other words of distress: "broken," "lost," and more bluntly, "screwed."

Pollsters say grouping people's answers together with synonyms and related words is a better reflection of public sentiment. Viewed that way, "struggling," "declining" and their synonyms accounted for the biggest chunk of words, from about one-fifth of answers. Some 18 percent of respondents offered words related to American greatness, prosperity and power, which collectively ranked second, followed by those linked to freedom (15 percent), and "confused," "lost" and similar choices (10 percent).

Positive and negative words were almost evenly split.

"When you see words like 'freedom' and 'divided' together, you get a good little portrait of what people are thinking," said Peter Sokolowski, editor-at-large at Merriam-Webster, the dictionary publisher. "You can't get more balanced than that."

Republicans used "struggling," "declining" and similar terms more than Democrats (27 percent versus 15 percent). Those without college degrees were also likelier to do so.

Bobby Underwood, a 67-year-old retired carpet mill worker in Dalton, Georgia, chose "troubled" when challenged to describe his country. With killings of police officers, Islamic State group attacks, a divisive election and concerns about the economy and illegal immigration, Underwood said he was left with an unhappy word in his mind.

"Troubled," he said. "That pretty much sums it up for me."

More than 350 individual words flowed into the poll released this week — from "bossy," "boring," "bountiful" and "bigoted" to "eclectic," "enthusiastic" and "equal." Also: "paradise," "perplexing," and a few cases of profanity. They pointed to high ideals — "democracy," "opportunity," "liberty" — and dire assessments — "greedy," "racist," and "doomed." Some screamed in all capital letters: "UNITED" and "TERRIFIED." Others used punctuation for added effect — "disaster!!" and "great!"

Jack Blanton of Lexington, Kentucky, thought of his 81 years in weighing his answer. He grew up in a rural town in the Appalachian foothills, working on his grandparents' tobacco farm and later in a steel mill. He moved around the country and saw the world, earned a Ph.D., and rose to become a university vice president.

He wondered what other country could give a farm boy such a life, and concluded America's best days are ahead. He decided on "great."

"Who wouldn't be optimistic?" he asked. "My whole life has been blessed."

America seen from abroad
Arrogant, nice, tech-savvy, free

For as far as I can remember I have straddled two cultures. Growing up in India, immersed in Indian folklore, history, ancient rituals and controlled chaos, I also lived vicariously an American life through American books and movies. And there were the Levis jeans, Wrigley chewing gum and tales of prosperity in the faraway land brought back by friends fortunate enough to travel. And I was not alone. Millions of middle-class Indians felt the same. When I became an adult and visited other countries I realized that many in other parts of the world were similarly bi-cultural.

So I excitedly said yes when my editors at the AP asked me if I would anchor a story on how the rest of the world views America at a time when America itself feels it is deeply divided. I felt I was eminently qualified. But things had changed from 40 years ago when I first became acquainted with the United States. It had been involved in several military interventions and was generally seen as a bully and a hypocrite. But to ensure that we didn't inject any unintended bias in our reporting we devised a set of five neutral questions that we hoped would provoke honest answers.

In the responses, elicited during dozens of interviews around the world, emerged a dominant theme – America had still not lost its sheen. Even among those who unlike me had very little exposure to the United States. While many were critical of the U.S. government, they still had a kindly view of America in general. If Americans see themselves as deeply divided, that was too bad. If they felt America needs to become great again, that was too bad. For the rest of the world, it was already great.
—Vijay Joshi, AP News Director, Southeast Asia

* * *

The rest of the world may think Americans eat a lot of burgers, have huge shopping malls and are ruled by an arrogant government. And yet the "Ugly American," it would seem, isn't all bad. Americans are also seen from afar as generous tippers, friendly, uncomplicated, rich and the standard bearers of freedom, equality, creativity and technological power.

While many Americans feel their nation is divided as never before, a sampling of the rest of the world reflects a more charitable view.

Generations in Asia, Africa, Europe and Latin America have grown up under the influence of the superpower U.S. and have felt awe and envy. America permeated their lives—through comics and Coke, through Hollywood and Neil Armstrong, and via the internet, iPhone and Facebook. It has been seen as the land of plenty, freedom and equality where Indian migrants could head behemoths like Google, Microsoft and Pepsi, and a South African could capture the imagination with an electric car. And after 9/11, the world grieved with America.

Yet, America's admirers have felt betrayed by other shades of the American character: the military interventions in Vietnam, Iraq and elsewhere; the gun violence; the right (inexplicable to many) to carry weapons; the deep and angry racial divisions; and, lately, a presidential nominee calling for harsh restrictions on Muslims and Mexicans.

The Associated Press sent reporters across the world to ask ordinary people about their views of America. And in the opinions that came back, some clear threads emerge, anecdotal yet illuminating.

WHAT IS THE FIRST THOUGHT THAT COMES TO MIND WHEN YOU HEAR THE WORD "AMERICA"?

"The first word that comes to mind when I hear the word America is 'Arrogance.' They are big and loud and they are in charge of everything."—Christopher Darroch, 39, actor, Toronto.

"Capitalism. Money rules everything. Overweight people, Donald Trump, elections, shootings."—Ingerlise Kristensen, 68, retired bank employee, Copenhagen, Denmark.

"America is food . . . fast food and (Coca) Cola. It's cars. It's the many electronics we have . . . the bridge in San Francisco."—Ksenia Smertova, 21, student, Moscow.

"America? Uhh, that's a huge country. Burgers, the American dream, choppers, . . . Elvis, cowboys. We dream of America and they dream about Europe. But one thing for sure, they cannot make beer."—Knut Braaten, 43, handyman, Oslo, Norway.

"Everything in America is high tech!"—B.S. Mehta, 34, health insurance agent, New Delhi.

"Has a very liberal culture, great people and a country that drives innovation."—Shitij, 26, sales and marketing worker, New Delhi.

"A lot of (consumer) products. A lot of dresses, and cars, and all that. A society that has more things than our society."—Antara Rao, 18, economics student, New Delhi.

Ayumi Takeoka, 41, says her image of America is positive, citing President Barack Obama's visit to Hiroshima. "I was delighted to see Obama-san came to Hiroshima and made that wonderful speech," she said. (AP Photo/Eugene Hoshiko)

"(America) welcomes all different races."—Marren Cahilig, 21, bartender, Manila, Philippines.

"It is powerful."—Gennelyn Escopete, 33, DVD street vendor, Manila, Philippines

"Probably capitalism, but I see it more as freedom . . . that every person can do what he wants, when he wants—true freedom, but it costs a lot I think, and sometimes it brings you lower than takes you higher."—Karin Cohen, 25, bookshop worker, Jerusalem.

"The first thing I think when I hear United States is a world power."—Pedro Ivan Gonzalez, 35, juice seller, Havana.

"It is a world imperialist power country. Obviously (the people) don't have much to do with the government's political decisions but I do think that it is a big, powerful country that has always tried to dominate countries it doesn't favor."—Rosa Moscoso, 42, Havana.

"A country of freedom, particularly freedom of thought. And it's a country with quite advanced technology industries. You see, I even have two iPhones."—Liu Xiaodan, 30, hotel manager, Beijing.

"America is a country that produces a massive amount of cultural output such as Hollywood movies, music and many other (forms of) entertainment."—Sam Wang, 20, university student, Beijing.

"My image of America is a country that goes to war anywhere in the world,"—Susumu Inoue, 82, retired agricultural lab technician, Tokyo.

"I think of Major League Baseball," Ayumi Takeoka, 41, housewife, Tokyo.

TALK ABOUT ONE EXPERIENCE YOU'VE HAD WITH AMERICA OR AN AMERICAN:

"I have been in the States a few times . . . It is a great country and would love to live there. People are nice but superficial. Not sure whether I actually am ready to move there because it must be a tough country to live in. I prefer it here. It is more cozy (laughing), less restrictive . . . (made drinking gesture)."—Knut Braaten, 43, handyman, Oslo, Norway.

"When I was driving to North Carolina I stopped at McDonald's. I was wearing a T-shirt that said, 'You Can't Get This In The States.' The fellow in line asked me in a very American accent, 'Y'all can't get what in the States?' I explained it was a joke, I was from Canada. And he said, 'Oh Canada! Y'all get snow up there.'"—Christopher Darroch, 39, actor, Toronto.

"I was stunned to see how big everything is over there. Shopping malls, meals, people, cars. We in Europe have smaller things . . . What I liked when I was over there was the service level, it was very high. But people expect to be tipped so that is why they are so services-minded. Their approach is different from ours . . . we do it because we care about others, they do it

Kanti, 74, owner of a travel agency, poses for a photograph in New Delhi, India. "I have traveled all over the United States in Greyhound buses as a tourist. I did not find any discrimination. I found the people . . . very hospitable, nice and very cordial," he says. (AP Photo/Tsering Topgyal)

because they get tips . . . they were raised that way."—Ingerlise Kristensen, 68, retired bank employee, Copenhagen, Denmark.

"I had a roommate . . . a Californian, when I was in Korea as a college exchange student. She was a happy person, better than my Chinese roommate . . . there were three of us in the room. The American was easy to talk with and we had a lot of things in common. (She believed) that the people's voice should be heard."—Marren Cahilig, 21, bartender, Manila, Philippines.

"A friend had an American friend over and he was surprised to see how laid back we are. He also emptied my friend's fridge, saying he's used to eating and drinking whenever he feels hungry or thirsty. And he drank tap water . . . oh no!"—Kenni Friis, 28, computer technology student, Copenhagen, Denmark.

"They're generous. If we ask for a high price, they don't bargain. They're calm and kind and friendly and they like to smile."—Gennelyn Escopete, 33, DVD street vendor, Manila, Philippines

"There is a lot of misconception about their politics. I've seen that many times they are very charismatic, friendly but that does not mean that they share the political thinking of the United States (government)."—Pedro Ivan Gonzalez, 35, Havana.

"I think the way they are talking and dealing with personal relations is quite direct. They just like speaking their mind, which is a reason that I don't feel quite comfortable going around with Americans."—Liu Xiaodan, 30, hotel manager, Beijing.

"My impression of Americans is that they uncomplicated. Interpersonal relations among Americans are much more practical, in contrast to the complicated way that we Chinese people treat each other."—Men Xuezhi, 54, doctor, Beijing.

"I don't like American guys who always pursue their own personal interests. I prefer hanging out with Canadians or students from Europe, because at least they are quite polite."—Li Jiaqi, 23, college student in U.S., renewing his visa in Beijing.

"An American friend visiting . . . came with the idea that he is going to find another America here . . . I believe they should understand the values that we have as Arabs, embrace them and try to go to a more local level to comprehend why we think and why we live the way we live."—Summer Abu Ltaif, outside the American University of Beirut.

"I think everyone is very tolerant there, in a way that there are all kinds of people, whether from different ethnicities, different countries, different religions. People are mostly not concerned with what another (person) is doing. There was a bit of a culture shock when I first went there because the way people dress there is very much different from the way we dress here. All of them wear shorts."—Antara Rao, 18, student, New Delhi.

"I have traveled all over the United States in Greyhound buses as a tourist. I did not find any discrimination. I found the people . . . very hospitable, nice and very cordial."—Kanti, 74, travel agency owner, New Delhi.

WHAT MAKES AMERICANS AMERICAN? OR WHAT IDENTIFIES AS AMERICAN TO YOU?

"A black-and-white look at the world. They miss nuances."—Knut Braaten, 43, handyman, Oslo, Norway.

"I think there obviously is the American dream, the idea that unifies them all. They are also unified in the sense that the dream isn't really a real thing anymore. The reality doesn't match the ideal. What identifies an American? Loudness. All of the Trump stuff in the U.S. has been depressing . . . you would like to think people are smarter than that . . . but definitely surprising and depressing to see how much support he has and how much support his ideas have."—Christopher Darroch, 39, actor, Toronto.

"Americans are American because they feel (they are) better than the rest of the world but in reality we are as good as they are. They simply don't see us as their equal . . . but we are. Sometimes we are even better than them. But don't tell them (laughing)."—Kenni Friis, 28, computer technology student, Copenhagen, Denmark.

"You can easily distinguish an American like here in the restaurant. The Americans are more of a tipper, good tippers. Americans are gallant."—Marren Cahilig, 21, bartender, Manila, Philippines.

"Many things . . . their arrogant ideology of a powerful country and above all they have a language that is practically universal and almost everyone depends on that language. And they are a people that like having a lot of fun . . . and their brands: McDonald's, all of that, makes the American identity . . . or North American . . . we call them North Americans rather than Americans, because we all are Americans."—Pedro Ivan Gonzalez, 35, Havana.

"Technology makes Americans American."—B.S. Mehta, 34, health insurance worker, New Delhi.

Sam Wang, 20, a university student, stands outside the U.S. embassy in Beijing, July 29, 2016. "America is a country that produces a massive amount of cultural output such as Hollywood movies, music and many other (forms of) entertainment," he says. (AP Photo/Mark Schiefelbein)

"America is a land of opportunities. I think that anybody with good ideas, if they want to make a mark, it gives you an equal opportunity in that country. America stands out because people recognize merit out there."—Shitij, 26, sales and marketing worker, New Delhi.

"They believe in democracy, in freedom; they are willing to die, kill, et cetera, for that. They believe in the right to have a good life and to help others to have a good life, and I think that's part of what makes them Americans."—Ziva Meizels, retiree, Jerusalem.

"I think their patriotism, you know, God bless America. And it is a great country; I have visited it. It's a wonderful country and there is high security, standard of living is very high. So yes, they are fortunate, and it is God bless America—that's what makes America, America."—Summer Abu Ltaif, outside the American University of Beirut.

"I think that they are formed by an ideology. There are no Americans as such. Because there is no such ethnicity. But there is an ideology that unites them all." —Zhila Gudzueva, university lecturer, Moscow.

"My definition of Americans is those who are cheerful, friendly and willing to communicate." —Ayumi Takeoka, 41, housewife, Tokyo.

Tempers and Temperatures Rise

Science is usually emotionless cut-and-dried facts, data and experiments. This is a story that was about science but it was about stuff that science has harder time quantifying and dealing with: feelings, a sense of what tribe you belong to and who you are. When we're talking about how the public views climate change, it's as much about the heart as the head. It's not just numbers about higher temperatures and rising seas, it's about what it does to people, their families, their friendships. The story of the Joyner family where a loving family is so publicly polarized over an issue that scientists say isn't up for debate tore at my heart. I liked everyone in the family. I hated to see them split so much. It hurt to hear Bob Inglis talk about how a close friend who used to come over to his house for monthly Bible study shun

him because of his stance on climate science and the same goes with Judy Curry who feels shunned from the science community.

Physics, chemistry and meteorology is supposed to explain, not cause pain. And yet what we do with or about the science shows the best and worst in people. Scientists shared hateful emails, Facebook posts and tweets. Those on the other side talked of being ridiculing. I've gotten my share of those nasty notes. You can lose faith in humanity.

And yet I come back to the Joyner family. No matter how much they disagree, no matter how much they argue, they still try to see eye to eye. They still love each other. So even this story is about how polarizing global warming has become, it's still one of hope.

—Seth Borenstein, AP Science Writer

* * *

Tempers are rising in America, along with the temperatures.

Two decades ago, the issue of climate change wasn't as contentious. The leading U.S. Senate proponent of taking action on global warming was Republican John McCain. George W. Bush wasn't as zealous on the issue as his Democratic opponent for president in 2000, Al Gore, but he, too, talked of regulating carbon dioxide.

Then the Earth got even hotter, repeatedly breaking temperature records. But instead of drawing closer together, politicians polarized.

Democrats (and scientists) became more convinced that global warming was a real, man-made threat. But Republicans and Tea Party activists became more convinced that it was—to quote the repeated tweets of presidential nominee Donald Trump—a "hoax." A Republican senator tossed a snowball on the Senate floor for his proof.

When it comes to science, there's more than climate that divides America's leaders and people. The mainstream scientific establishment accepts evolution as a reality, as well as the general safety of vaccinations and genetically modified food. But some political leaders and portions of the public don't believe any of that. It's not a liberal versus conservative issue, especially when it comes to vaccinations, which are doubted by some activists on both ends of the political spectrum.

But nothing beats climate change for divisiveness.

"It's more politically polarizing than abortion," says Anthony Leiserowitz, director of the Yale Program on Climate Change Communication. "It's more politically polarizing than gay marriage."

Leiserowitz says 17 percent of Americans, the fastest-growing group, are alarmed by climate change and want action now, based on surveys by Yale and George Mason University.

Another 28 percent are concerned, thinking it's a man-made threat, but somewhat distant in time and place. Twenty-seven percent are cautious, still on the fence, and 11 percent are doubtful. An often-vocal 10 percent are dismissive, rejecting the concept of warming and the science. And about 7 percent are disengaged, not even paying attention because they've got more pressing needs.

So while the largest group is at least concerned with climate change, significant segments are not. And sometimes those segments mix in one family.

Rick and Julie Joyner of Fort Mill, South Carolina, are founders of MorningStar ministries. Most of the people they associate with reject climate change. Their 31-year-old daughter, Anna Jane, is a climate change activist.

Rick Joyner, 66, would visit New York with other evangelicals to meet with Trump and then hear a completely different world view from his daughter.

As part of a documentary a few years ago, Anna Jane introduced Rick to scientists who made the case for climate change. It did not work. He labels himself more skeptical than before.

"They're both stubborn and equally entrenched in their positions," says Julie, who is often in the middle. "It doesn't get ugly too often."

TRIBALISM

Recall the 20th century, with its race to the moon, advances in medicine and information technology, and "this incredibly strong belief in the promise of science," says Matthew Nisbet, a communications professor at Northeastern University.

People in the 1960s "had faith in science, had hope in science. Most people thought science was responsible for improving their daily lives," says Marcia McNutt, president of the National Academy of Sciences.

So some scientists look back at that era with nostalgia, she says.

That's because now, Nisbet says, "we see partisan polarization or ideological polarization" and the implications of science "are intuitively recognized as threatening to one side and their world view."

Yale psychology and law professor Dan Kahan argues, however, that public divides on science have existed for decades. He notes that some issues that formerly divided us no longer do, such as the dangers of cigarettes, after a public health campaign eroded the social acceptability of smoking.

The split with science is most visible and strident when it comes to climate change because the nature of the global problem requires communal joint action, and "for conservatives that's especially difficult to accept," Nisbet says.

Climate change is more about tribalism, or who we identify with politically and socially, Nisbet and other experts say. Liberals believe in global warming, conservatives don't.

Dave Woodard, a Clemson University political science professor and GOP consultant, helped South Carolina Republican Bob Inglis run for the U.S. House (successfully) and the Senate (unsuccessfully). They'd meet monthly at Inglis' home for Bible study, and were in agreement that global warming wasn't an issue and probably was not real.

"I said climate change was nonsense, Al Gore's imagination," Inglis says.

After seeing the effects of warming first-hand in Antarctica and Australia's Great Barrier Reef, Inglis changed his mind—and was overwhelmingly defeated in a GOP primary in 2010. Woodard helped run the campaign that beat him and hasn't been to his former friend's home for about a decade.

"I was seen as crossing to the other side, as helping the Al Gore tribe, and that could not be forgiven," Inglis says.

Woodward responds that the new Bob Inglis didn't fit South Carolina.

"If you want to talk climate change, you need to go up to New York and Boston to do that. You don't talk that down here," he says. "Conservatives just don't believe. They think it's like Martians."

Judy Curry, a Georgia Tech atmospheric scientist and self-described climate gadfly, has experienced ostracism from the other side. She repeatedly

Scientist Oliver Grah measures the speed of a melt water stream from Sholes Glacier on one of the slopes on Mount Baker in Washington. Since 1997, the world has warmed by 0.44 degrees (0.25 degrees Celsius) and 51 monthly or annual global heat records were broken, according to the National Oceanic and Atmospheric Administration. (AP Photo/Manuel Valdes)

clashed with former colleagues after she publicly doubted the extent of global warming and criticized the way mainstream scientists operate. Now she says, no one will even look at her for other jobs in academia.

"What's wrong with disagreement? People disagree. You listen or you don't," Curry says. "This polarization comes down to being intolerant on disagreement."

WHAT CHANGED

In 1997, then-Vice President Gore helped broker an international treaty, the Kyoto Protocol, to reduce heat-trapping gases from the burning of coal, oil and gas. The U.S. later withdrew from the treaty.

"And at that moment" says Leiserowitz, "the two parties begin to divide. They begin to split and go farther and farther and farther apart until we reach today's environment where climate change is now one of the most polarized issues in America."

The election of Barack Obama and the Tea Party revolt made the schism even bigger, he says.

Stanford University's Jon Krosnick agrees that things changed around 1997, but he thinks Americans are fairly united—it's just they don't realize it. Krosnick's surveys show that nearly 90 percent of Democrats, 80 percent of independents and 70 percent of Republicans believe the increase in world's temperature over the past century was mostly or partly caused by humans.

His studies show fairly consistent numbers, except for a drop in Republicans to 50 percent in 2011 that since has returned to 70 percent.

A bigger split in Stanford surveys indicates that while about 90 percent of Democrats and 80 percent of independents believe global warming will be a serious or very serious problem for the United States, barely half of Republicans feel that way.

To illustrate how the issue plays out in all sorts of ways, let's take lobster scientist Diane Cowan in Friendship, Maine, who expresses dismay.

"I am definitely bearing witness to climate change," Cowan says. "I read about climate change. I knew sea level was rising but I saw it and, until it impacted me directly, I didn't feel it the same way."

Republican Jodi Crosson, a 55-year-old single mother and production and sales manager in Bexley, Ohio, thinks global warming is a serious problem because she's felt the wrath of extreme weather and rising heat. But to her, it's not quite as big an issue as the economy.

And then there's Ken Martig Jr. An engineer and business owner in Allyn, Washington, he paid little attention to global warming until he learned that one proposed solution involved regulations and taxes. Now he doesn't think climate change is man-made or a major worry.

"If you put it down to one word today, it's a trust issue," the 73-year-old Martig says. "Do you really know for a fact that it's burning of the (fossil) fuels that are creating these greenhouse gases" that are causing the world to warm?

Scott Tiller, a 59-year-old underground coal miner in West Virginia, has seen mine after mine close, and he agrees with Martig.

"I think we've been treated unfairly and kind of looked down upon as polluters," Tiller says. "They say the climate is changing, but are we doing it? Or is it just a natural thing that the Earth does?"

BRIDGING DIFFERENCES

Overwhelmingly, scientists who study the issue say it is man-made and a real problem. Using basic physics and chemistry and computer simulations, scientists have repeatedly calculated how much extra warming is coming from natural forces and how much comes from humans. The scientists and their peer-reviewed research blame human activity, for the most part.

Dozens of scientific measurements show Earth is warming. Since 1997, the world has warmed by 0.44 degrees (0.25 degrees Celsius) and 51 monthly or annual global heat records were broken, according to the National Oceanic and Atmospheric Administration.

Arctic sea ice, ice sheets and glaciers are melting faster. The seas have risen and hot water has been killing coral in record numbers. Scientists have connected man-made climate change to extreme weather, including deadly heat waves, droughts and flood-inducing downpours. Allergies, asthma and pest-borne diseases are worsening public health problems, with experts blaming climate change.

A farmer holds a piece of his drought- and heat-stricken corn while chopping it down for feed in Nashville, IL. Scientists have connected man-made climate change to extreme weather, including deadly heat waves, droughts and flood-inducing downpours. (AP Photo/Seth Perlman)

Scientists keep acting as if they just do a better job showing data or teaching, then people can understand that climate change is a problem—and that's just not the way people work, says Yale's Kahan.

He points to polling showing that if you ask people if scientists are sure global warming is real, man-made and a threat, they'll say yes.

"They know that scientists say we're screwed," Kahan says. "But it's not what activates them."

Twice in the last seven years, scientific societies sent group letters to Congress explaining that warming is real, man-made threat.

"I honestly believe that low science literacy allows people to fall for things that make no sense," says University of Georgia meteorology professor Marshall Shepherd. "For example, when it is cold or a snowy day, I may get a comment like 'There is 20 inches of global warming in my yard.' While that is a cute, snarky comment, it really illustrates a lack of understanding of weather versus climate."

Kahan says the most ardent doubters of climate change are also among the best-educated groups on the science—along with the most ardent believers. They are driven by ideology, he says.

So instead of spouting statistics, some climate activists and even scientists try to build bridges to communities that might doubt that the Earth is warming but are not utterly dismissive.

The more people connect on a human level, the more people can "overcome these tribal attitudes," Anna Jane Joyner says. "We really do have a lot more in common than we think."

Disagreement is OK, says her father, Rick.

"True unity is not a unity in conformity, but a unity in diversity," he says. "We look at differences as an opportunity to learn, not to divide."

Diverse millennials are no voting monolith

In popular culture, the millennial generation has generally been disparaged as self-obsessed, indulgent and lazy.

Demographics experts told me in early interviews, however, that one thing that isn't well understood about this generation is how much they have been influenced by the historical events that shaped their young lives: the Sept. 11, 2001 terror attacks, the Great Recession, foreign wars and the digital revolution. One researcher I interviewed said their coming-of-age experience most parallels those who grew up in the 1920s, an era of rapid technological innovation bookended by wars and ravaged by the Great Depression.

When he said that, I didn't take it seriously. Selfie-obsessed millennials on a par with their great-grandparents? I didn't see it. But as our team delved into the reporting work, I was struck by how often those key historical events played into our subjects' world view, their politics and into the very core of who they were.

It turns out they care deeply about politics. They just don't talk about it as much, or in ways we expect.

Trump supporters cited the economic turmoil they witnessed as a reason for support-ing him, but those backing Clinton also cited that as a reason for their choice. Others told us they were starting out their adults lives tens of thousands of dollars in debt from college. One 21-year-old interviewee said the only time she could ever remember America feeling united was the day after Sept. 11, 2001 — when she was 7.

It was a revealing statement, and one that I thought about a lot as I reported and wrote the story with my colleagues Tamara Lush and Martha Irvine. As a Gen Xer myself, I grew up in an era of relative peace and prosperity and the realities these young Americans faced seemed alien to me. I came away with a much greater understanding of and respect for our youngest American citizens, and a greater empathy for the world they grew up in _ the only one they have known.

I hope our story did that for readers as well. Because soon, these millennial voters will be the nation's parents and grandparents, the ones who shape our collective future and they have a lot to say.

—Gillian Flaccus, AP Reporter, Portland, OR

* * *

The oldest millennials—nearing 20 when airplanes slammed into New York City's Twin Towers—are old enough to remember the relative economic prosperity of the 1990s, and when a different Clinton was running for pres-ident. The nation's youngest adults—now nearing 20 themselves—find it hard to recall a reality without terrorism and economic worry.

Now millennials have edged out baby boomers as the largest living generation in U.S. history, and more than 75 million of them have come of age. How they vote on Nov. 8 will shape the political landscape for years to come. Yet with less than three months to go before Election Day, the values of young Americans whose coming-of-age was bookended by the Sept. 11, 2001, terrorist attacks and the Great Recession are emerging as an unpredictable grab bag of fiscal conservatism and social liberalism.

What they share is a palpable sense of disillusionment.

The Associated Press spent time with seven millennial voters in five states where the oldest and largest swath of this generation—ages 18 to 35, as defined by the Pew Research Center—could have an outsized influence in November. They are a uniquely American mosaic, from a black teen in Nevada voting for the first time to a Florida-born son of Latino immigrants to a white Christian couple in Ohio.

Taken individually, these voters illustrate how millennials are challenging pollsters' expectations based on race, class and background in surprising ways, reacting to what they see as the loss of the American Dream. They are intent on shaping something new and important that reflects their reality— on their own terms.

"Millennials have been described as apathetic, but they're absolutely not. I think you can see from this election year that they're not, and that millennials have a very nuanced understanding of the political world," said Diana Downard, a 26-year-old Bernie Sanders supporter who will vote for Hillary Clinton. "So yeah, I'm proud to be a millennial."

Just 5 percent of young adults say that America is "greater than it has ever been," while 52 percent feel the nation is "falling behind" and 24 percent believe the U.S. is "failing," according to a GenForward poll released last month. The first-of-its kind survey of young people between the ages of 18 and 30 was conducted by the Black Youth Project at the University of Chicago with the Associated Press-NORC Center for Public Affairs Research.

Fifty-four percent believe only a few people at the top can get ahead in today's America, and 74 percent say income and wealth distribution are uneven, according to the poll.

Briana Lawrence, a 21-year-old videographer and eyelash artist from Durham, North Carolina, identifies with those numbers.

She was just 7 on Sept. 11 and the immediate aftermath of the terrorist attacks is the only time she can remember the nation feeling united, even if only by grief. With $40,000 in student debt, she's working hard to establish her own cosmetic business after graduating from North Carolina Central University. She plans to vote for Hillary Clinton, but feels America has lost its way.

Briana Lawrence, 21, a Hillary Clinton supporter, in a studio at North Carolina Central University in Durham, NC, July 14, 2016. (AP Photo/Gerry Broome)

"My biggest hope for this country is for us to come back together as a community. As a United States of America, to unite together again," she said.

But millennials know that getting to that place won't be easy. Many, like Lawrence, are saddled with college debt and have struggled to find jobs.

In Denver, 1,600 miles to the west, Downard also has almost $40,000 in student debt that's already changed her path. A dual U.S. and Mexican citizen, she feels she can't afford to work for an overseas organization—one of her dreams—and plans to delay having a family at least 10 years. "We went to college in pursuit of a better life and really, now, we're kind of just paralyzed by our student debt," said Downard, who works for a non-partisan organization that works to improve youth voter registration. "You can't even think about those sorts of alternative options."

In part because of these economic pressures, a 2014 Pew Research Center poll found that—for the first time in more than 130 years—adults ages 18 to 34 were slightly more likely to be living with their parents than with a spouse or partner in their own residence. And one in four millennials say they might not ever marry, a Pew survey found.

Only 8 percent of young adults feel their household's financial situation is "very good," and education and economic growth ranked No. 1 and No. 2 as the issues that will most influence their vote, according to the GenForward poll.

"We might be in a 'good-ish' finance situation right now as a country, but I was always taught there's ups and downs in the finance world and with every up, there's a down. So we should be preparing for that down to come," said Brien Tillett, who graduated this spring from a high school just miles from the Las Vegas Strip.

Tillett, who turned 18 in July, was 10 when the recession hit and sucked the wind out of his family. His mother, a single parent, was in a car accident that hospitalized her for three months and, with no safety net, the family struggled.

"It was to the point where I would not ask my mother to go hang out with my friends because I didn't want her to worry about money," said Tillett, whose brush with insolvency has deeply influenced his views.

The national debt is his No. 1 concern.

As a young black man, he's turned off by remarks by Donald Trump that he finds racist and xenophobic, but likes Trump's aggressive stance on the economy. "We're trillions of dollars in debt and that should not be happening," said Tillett, who started running track at a two-year college this month.

He strongly considered voting for Trump, but will now vote for Clinton because Trump has become "a loose cannon" in recent weeks. Still, he's angry about Clinton's use of a private email server when she was Secretary of State. "We have to basically question if we can truly trust her with all of our nation's secrets," he said.

Anibal David Cabrera was in high school when Tillett was just a small boy—but he's part of the same generation.

The son of a Honduran mother and Dominican father, he graduated from college in 2008 as the recession was picking up steam. A finance major, he wanted to work for a hedge fund or bank, but the economic collapse meant jobs had dried up. Eventually Cabrera, now 31 and living in Tampa, Florida, got an accounting job at a small tech firm.

He feels he's entering the prime of his life a few steps behind where he could have been, through no fault of his own.

A Jeb Bush die-hard in the primaries, he's now supporting Trump and hopes the business mogul can make good on his promises.

"My biggest hope for the country would be a prosperous economy. That is something my generation has kind of never seen," Cabrera said. "We never got to experience the rapid growth of the '80s or the '90s, and I think my generation would love to see that."

Shared pain does not lead to shared views among his generation.

Millennial voters' disdain for traditional party affiliation has made them particularly unpredictable. Half describe themselves as political independents, according to a 2014 Pew Research report—a near-record level of political disaffiliation. As a generation, they tend to be extremely liberal on social questions such as gay marriage, abortion and marijuana legalization. Yet they skew slightly conservative on fiscal policy and are more in line with other generations on gun control and foreign affairs.

Trip Nistico, a recent graduate of the University of Colorado, Boulder's law school, is an avid supporter of gun rights who goes to shooting ranges

Trip Nistico, 26, a Donald Trump supporter, is an avid supporter of gun rights who goes to shooting ranges but also supports same-sex marriage, Boulder, CO, July 5, 2016. (AP Photo/Brennan Linsley)

but also supports same-sex marriage. The 26-year-old Texas native voted for President Barack Obama in 2008—his first presidential election—and Mitt Romney in 2012.

"I'm pretty liberal on social issues. I don't really think that—on a national level—they're really as important as some of these other issues we've been discussing," he said.

He's supporting Trump because his preferred candidate, the Libertarian Party's Gary Johnson, isn't likely to crack the polls.

Trump remains wildly unpopular among young adults, however, and nearly two-thirds of Americans between the ages of 18 and 30 believe the Republican nominee is racist, according to the GenForward poll. Views of Hillary Clinton also were unfavorable, though not nearly to the same extent.

Many millennials are angry that Democratic challenger Bernie Sanders has withdrawn and are disillusioned with the electoral process.

Forty-two percent of voters under 30 have "hardly any confidence" that the Republican presidential nomination process is fair and 38 percent feel the same about the Democratic process, according to the GenForward poll. The survey was taken before the leak of Democratic National Committee emails that roiled the Democratic Party.

Bill and Kristi Clay, young parents and devout Christians from rural Ohio, offer a portrait of millennials struggling to choose a candidate who matches their values.

They have two sons, 4 and 6, and are adopting a child from the Philippines. They serve meals with their church at inner-city soup kitchens in nearby Columbus and have a mix of political views that, Bill Clay says, comes from following "the lamb, not the donkey or elephant."

Kristi Clay opposes same-sex marriage and abortion and names those as her top issues this election. Yet the 32-year-old school librarian is still reluctantly leaning toward voting for Clinton. "You have to look at the big picture," she says.

Bill Clay, meanwhile, shares his wife's views on the more conservative issues, but they hold what some would consider more liberal views on matters such as immigration.

"If we're going to try to be Christian-like, and embrace people, I don't think you can shut the borders to an entire group of people just because

Pictures of children sponsored by Bill Clay and his wife, Kristi, are displayed on their refrigerator as they prepare breakfast for their children, Ami, left, and Xavier at their home in Ashville, OH, July 9, 2016. (AP Photo/John Minchillo)

of the fear that some of them don't like us," said Clay, 33, who voted for Barack Obama in the last two elections but supported Republican Marco Rubio this time.

Yet that strong faith has not helped him find much inspiration in the current candidates, both of whom he sees as self-serving and unwilling to budge on important issues.

"I'm feeling a little pessimistic this year," he said.

The Clays say they will vote no matter what, but whether their millennial brothers and sisters do the same is an open question.

The millennial vote rose steadily beginning in 2002 and peaked in 2008, with excitement over Obama's first campaign. In 2012, however, just 45 percent of millennials cast ballots and participation has leveled off or dropped ever since, said John Della Volpe, director of polling at Harvard University's Institute of Politics.

"They have a somewhat different perspective in terms of politics, "Della Volpe said. "It hasn't really worked. They haven't been part of a movement that's been effective."

Yet Tillett, the teen in Nevada, exudes youthful idealism as he talks about casting his first vote in a presidential election.

"It means a lot to me personally because I'm making a difference in my life and in the country. My vote does matter," he said. "It really does."

Will Trump energize the Latino vote?

Because Donald Trump kicked off his campaign insulting Mexican immigrants, political stories for the past year have been chock full of references to the Latino vote. It's almost become a form of magical thinking: Trump can't win because he insulted Latinos. The Latino vote will stop him.

My colleague Sergio Bustos and I wanted to dig deeper. Actually getting Latinos to vote in the overwhelming numbers that, on paper, they're capable of is hard, expensive and exhausting work. It's not something that happens automatically. And because of immigration status and age, many Latinos are shut out of the political process — stuck on the sidelines as the nation debates their families' futures.

Trump may have helped turn out Latinos, but he may also demonstrate why the nation's largest minority group still can't change the outcome of this election.
—Nicholas Riccardi, AP Western Political Writer

* * *

It's a persistent paradox in American politics: Many Hispanic families have an immense personal stake in what happens on Election Day, but despite population numbers that should mean political power, Hispanics often can't vote, aren't registered to vote, or simply choose to sit out.

Enter Donald Trump, and the question that could make or break this year's divisive presidential election in key states. By inflaming the anti-immigrant sentiments of white, working-class men, has the Republican nominee jolted awake another group—the now 27.3 million eligible Hispanic voters long labeled the sleeping giant of U.S. elections?

"A lot of times you hear this rap about how politics doesn't affect their life," says Yvanna Cancela, political director of Las Vegas' largely immigrant Culinary Union. "But that changes when it's personal, and there's nothing more personal than Donald Trump talking about deporting 11 million immigrants."

Hispanics now represent the nation's largest ethnic community with some 55 million people. More than half are U.S.-born, an additional 6.5 million are naturalized citizens, and the others are legal residents or here illegally. Most trace their familial roots to Mexico, one of Trump's favorite targets.

"When Mexico sends its people, they're not sending their best," Trump said last summer, minutes into the speech that announced his candidacy. "They're bringing drugs. They're bringing crime. They're rapists."

A cornerstone of Trump's platform is building a wall along the entire Southwest border—and forcing Mexico to pay for it. How? By threatening to cut off remittances those living in the U.S. send to relatives down south.

He publicly attacked and questioned the impartiality of an Indiana-born federal judge hearing a lawsuit against him because of the judge's Mexican ancestry. He's called protesters in New Mexico "thugs who were flying the Mexican flag" and accused the state's governor—a Republican who also happens to be the nation's first female Hispanic governor—of "not doing the job." Half of that state's population is Hispanic, as are 40 percent of the state's eligible voters.

This is hardly what the Republican National Committee had in mind three years ago when, after Mitt Romney's loss to Barack Obama, it commissioned a study about how best to bring more Hispanics, blacks, women and young voters into the fold. An entire section called "America Looks Different" urged Republicans to engage with minority voters, "show our sincerity" and "embrace and champion comprehensive immigration reform."

Skip ahead to 2016, and surveys that show most Hispanics plan to vote against the Republican nominee. A Fox News Latino poll conducted in May found 67 percent back Hillary Clinton and only 23 percent support Trump.

A sign in Spanish which translates, "Don't Lose Your Voice, Vote!" is displayed near a polling place in a Cardenas supermarket in Las Vegas, June 10, 2016. (AP Photo/John Locher)

John Herrera, 38, is typical. He registered to vote in Las Vegas in June. "I've never really voted until now, only because of Trump being against Hispanic people," he said. "I didn't think my vote would count before, but now I want to make a difference."

Lionel Sosa, a prominent Mexican-American advertising and marketing executive in San Antonio, was once dubbed one of the top 25 most influential Hispanics in America by Time magazine. He helped devise strategies to attract Latino voters for the likes of Ronald Reagan, George W. Bush and John McCain.

That was before Trump. In a June column in the San Antonio Express-News, Sosa announced he'd be leaving the party upon Trump's formal nomination.

"A thousand points of light has been replaced by a thousand points of anger. In place of compassionate conservatism, our nominee promotes callousness, extremism and racism. And instead of a unifier, the party now cheers the ultimate 'us against them' proponent. Divisiveness incarnate," he wrote.

Republican fears of Hispanic backlash are rooted in what happened after their party targeted illegal immigration in California in 1994.

Gov. Pete Wilson tied his re-election campaign to a ballot measure, Proposition 187, to deny government benefits and access to public schools to people in the country illegally. The measure passed, and though it was later struck down as unconstitutional, a growing Hispanic population was infuriated.

In the years since, more Latinos have been elected to office in the state and the GOP has dwindled to a mere footnote; no Republican has won a statewide election in California since 2006. Proposition 187 wasn't the only factor in the change—other groups in California, like coastal whites, were shifting Democratic in the mid-'90s, and Hispanics already leaned against the GOP. But the loss of California has become the example of the risk Republicans run alienating a fast-growing ethnic group.

"With Trump saying the things he's saying, we might see this same thing again," says Jody Agius Vallejo, a University of Southern California sociologist and author of "Barrios to Burbs: The Making of the Mexican American Middle Class." "Only this time, it would be nationally."

There is reason, though, to be skeptical. Overall, the Hispanic voting record is not good.

One obstacle is some 7.2 million Hispanic adults are here illegally and are ineligible to vote, according to estimates from the Pew Research Center. Another 5 million, while living here legally as temporary or permanent residents, are not citizens.

Finally, nearly one-third of all Hispanics in the U.S., some 17.9 million, are under age 18—young people like Edysmar Diaz-Cruz, a high school student from Miami, whose 18th birthday comes one month after the presidential contest.

"It's so disappointing because I've been closely following this year's campaign," she says.

Relatively few of the Hispanics who are eligible to vote actually register and then cast ballots. In the 2012 election, only 48 percent of eligible Hispanic voters turned out, according to the Pew Research Center. That's compared to a 66.6 percent turnout rate among blacks and a 64.1 percent rate among whites.

In Arizona, a decade of tough-on-immigration policies from Republican officials has triggered no popular uprising by the state's growing Hispanic population; the GOP still controls all state offices, and activists acknowledge that increasingly conservative white votes there tend to mitigate gains among Hispanics, who now represent about one-fifth of the state's voters.

In Texas, where 39 percent of the population is Hispanic, Democrats have been shut out of statewide elections for decades. During 2014's midterm elections, fewer than 2.3 million Texas Hispanics reported being registered to vote, or about 46 percent of the nearly 4.9 million who were eligible, according to U.S. Census Bureau surveys. Turnout was even worse: That year, 22 percent of eligible Texas Hispanics reported voting compared to nearly 42 percent of eligible whites and 35 percent of eligible blacks.

"We've been spending our money wrong," concedes Crystal Zermeno, director of special projects for the Democratic field organization Texas Organizing Project.

"For the past 15 to 20 years, we've been focusing on moving swing white voters. If you talk to Hispanic voters, they say, 'No one has asked me to vote,'" Zermeno says. "There has not been a focus and real expenditures historically on unlikely voters, and you can't just expect non-voters to go out in great numbers . . . without anyone encouraging them."

Unions, nonprofits and political campaigns have struggled to grow the Hispanic electorate, with mixed success.

In Colorado, Democratic groups have invested for years to reach out, and Hispanic registration and turnout have edged higher. In 2013, a state assembly that had been tough on illegal immigration allowed people in the country illegally to pay in-state tuition at public colleges and universities.

Crystal Zermeno, a supporter of Hillary Clinton, attends a Democratic National Convention watch party in San Antonio, July 26, 2016. (AP Photo/ Eric Gay)

Nevada is another battleground state, where some 17 percent of eligible voters, or 328,000 people, are Hispanics. Here, Latinos have clearly demonstrated the power they wield when they either turn out or stay home. In 2008 and 2012 they helped President Barack Obama; they were critical in re-electing Sen. Harry Reid in 2010. In the 2014 midterms, though, Hispanic turnout plummeted, and Republicans swept every statewide office and won control of both houses of the Legislature for the first time since 1929.

"When you have the resources put in, you see turnout that favors the Democrats," says David Damore, a political science professor at the University of Nevada Las Vegas. "But you need to put resources in the community. It's not just going to happen."

This year—with Trump priming the pump, and with former state Attorney General Catherine Cortez Masto running to replace the retiring Reid and become the first Latina senator—resources are flowing. Groups like Mi Familia Vota are sending in staff from around the country and hiring local volunteers to step up registration and turnout efforts.

In June, two days after graduating from high school, Fabiola Vejar stood outside a Latin grocery store on a sweltering afternoon quizzing a parade of customers in Spanish: "Are you registered to vote?" Most shook their heads no. Vejar followed up: "Are you eligible?" Again, most responded in the negative. One man laughed and bellowed: "Soy Mexicano!" I'm Mexican!

Vejar cannot vote. Now 18, she entered the country illegally from Mexico with her mother when she was 2 years old, after her father died of leukemia.

Her future, and that of her family, largely depends on this election. She is shielded from deportation under an Obama administration program that protects those brought to the country illegally as children. Hillary Clinton has promised to keep that program, and Trump to end it. Trump also has pledged to deport every person in the country illegally, and that would include not just Fabiola, but her mother and stepfather. Her two brothers are both U.S. citizens, but not yet 18.

So Vejar volunteers with Mi Familia Vota, encouraging others to be heard at the ballot box.

"I don't have that voice," she says, "but there's other people . . . who feel the way I do. They should vote."

Some, like Jose Martinez, are unconvinced. The 40-year-old security guard voted twice for Obama but told one of Vejar's colleagues he is sitting this election out because he's disappointed the president did not pass a broad immigration overhaul.

"He promised a lot, a lot to Latinos," Martinez says. "He did maybe 1 percent. . . . We don't believe in anything now."

Joe Enriquez Henry remembers the moment he set out to disprove the conventional wisdom that Hispanics just don't vote. It was 2002, and then-Iowa Gov. Tom Vilsack, a Democrat, signed a bill making English the state's official language. Vilsack now says he regrets the decision, but the governor then explained to Henry that Latinos just were too small a voting constituency to convince him to put down the pen.

Henry, whose mother's family came to the U.S. from Mexico more than 100 years ago, vowed he'd help Iowa's small but significant Hispanic population—now more than 170,000, or nearly 6 percent of the state's population—make their voices heard. Years of work paid off on Feb. 1, when as many as 13,000 Hispanics turned out for the state's caucuses. Only about 1,000 had attended in 2012.

"The Democratic and Republican parties think we don't vote, so we wanted to prove that we do," says Henry, a vice president of the League of United Latin American Citizens.

There was no magic formula. Henry scraped together $200,000 that paid for a few staffers who made phone calls, distributed fliers and knocked on doors to talk about the importance of voting with people like Mayra de Catalan, an immigrant from El Salvador who works as a bank analyst.

The Des Moines resident has been in the U.S. for two decades and became a citizen only five years ago; she says she had not even considered voting.

"It was the first time anyone had talked to me about the importance of voting," she says, "how my one vote could make a difference."

That's the same message that Victor Juarez is spreading in Nevada. He has been a member of Culinary Union Local 226 since 1989, when he started work as a cook at the Circus, Circus casino. The union represents 55,000 casino and hotel workers, half of them Hispanic and many of them

Members of the Culinary Union Local 226 celebrate as they hear results during a primary election in Las Vegas. Half of the union's predominantly-immigrant members are Hispanic and an electoral powerhouse, June 14, 2016. (AP Photo/John Locher)

immigrants; it has harnessed Las Vegas' housekeepers, cooks and janitors and turned them into an electoral powerhouse.

Juarez has been taking paid leaves of absence to work as an organizer for Culinary, traveling around town and knocking on doors of other union members to get them to the polls. He himself only became a citizen, able to vote, after the 2004 election; he was working two jobs to put his children through school and says he didn't have time.

Often he finds families headed by people with little education who don't speak English and are wary of participating in the system.

"We had to open their eyes," he says. "There's a lack of education, language barriers."

With Trump, he says, he has noticed a change. "People who've been living here a long time are getting scared about what he's saying."

Xiomara Duenas is one of them. She immigrated legally to the United States from Cuba in 1996 to join her father. She worked at a seafood processing plant in New Jersey before moving to Nevada in 2012 after medical issues forced an early retirement. She had always believed that her shaky English prevented her from becoming a citizen. She was resigned to the idea that immigrants didn't have the same rights as native-born Americans—until Trump's candidacy.

Duenas found a Culinary Union citizenship workshop where Spanish speakers guided her through the process.

Last November, she became a citizen. This November, she plans to act.

"I didn't want him to become president, but I couldn't do anything," says Duenas. "But now, I can vote."

....

Houston, Texas
Hispanic voting bloc largely untapped

by Will Weissert, AP Administrative Correspondent

Diana Villenas begins her pitch in English, but switches to Spanish if she gets blank stares, which happens often. It's a tough sell in any language.

"Are you registered to vote?" asks the 21-year-old environmental studies student at St. Thomas University in Houston. "Do you want to be?"

"No, gracias," the bearded man in the black baseball cap says. Another ambling by with a cellphone to his ear shakes his head, as does a guy in a black-felt cowboy hat and a woman wearing a yellow blouse. The man in an American flag T-shirt even turns her down.

As brassy Banda music blares from a nearby stage at a sprawling Hispanic festival adjacent to the Houston Texans' dome, Villenas and other volunteers with Mi Familia Vota, a nonpartisan nonprofit which encourages Latino civic engagement, exhort possible voters. They find most aren't eligible to vote because they've not yet turned 18 or are recent immigrants who aren't U.S. citizens.

Many others, though, simply aren't interested.

Texas is home to 10.2 million Hispanics, 19 percent of the country's Latino population. Excluding noncitizens and those under 18, about 5 million Texas Hispanics will be eligible to vote in the 2016 presidential election, but less than half may register and fewer still are likely to cast ballots.

Consider the 2014 midterm elections, when less than 2.3 million Texas Hispanics reported in U.S. Census surveys that they were registered to vote — about 46 percent of the nearly 4.9 million that were eligible and about 300,000 fewer than reported being registered in 2012. Turnout in 2014 was worse than 2012: 22 percent of eligible Texas Hispanics voted compared to 39 percent. Nationwide, 48 percent of Hispanics reported voting in 2012, which declined to 27 percent in 2014.

That untapped electorate helps explain how, even though a majority of the state's residents will be Hispanic by around 2030, Texas has grown increasingly conservative. No Democrat has won statewide office here since 1994, the country's longest political losing streak.

Some Hispanics support Texas conservative causes, such as religious values and opposing abortion, but overall, Latinos statewide still lean strongly Democratic, as do their counterparts elsewhere. Higher Latino turnout won't turn this red state blue in November's presidential election, but given how much the Hispanic population is booming, even small improvements could make a big difference in the future. The trick will be pulling that off.

"We should know that demography is not destiny," said Henry Munoz III, a longtime San Antonio community organizer who now serves as the Democratic Party's National Finance Committee Chair.

Hispanic voting habits are like church attendance, said Mario Salinas, Mi Familia Vota's deputy Texas director.

"If you grow up in a house where mom and dad go to church, you'll go too as an adult. If they don't, you probably won't," Salinas said. "If parents don't vote, the kids won't."

Texas ranks near the bottom nationally in total voter turnout, due in part to a heavily-under-30 population, which tends to vote less than elder counterparts.

Count Lesley Resendiz, a 20-year-old from Houston, among them. She is registered and said she knows how important it is for Hispanics to embrace voting, but that her work schedule kept her from doing so in the March primary.

"A lot of people I know use social media to talk about politics," Resendiz said. "But they don't vote because it's not as easy as just going online."

Across the country, naturalization applications are up 14 percent in the last six months of 2015 compared with the same period the previous year. That has fueled speculation that many Hispanics are anxious to vote against Donald Trump, fearful of the Republican nominee's harsh immigration rhetoric.

But Alberto Morales, project coordinator for the Advocacy Alliance Center of Texas, which leads voter registration drives along the Texas-Mexico border, cautions that it might not translate to higher turnout.

"There is frustration," Morales said. "We would just like for more of the population to come out to vote and they're just not."

Because Texas is so solidly Republican, neither Trump nor Democrat Hillary Clinton will focus on it for November's election, meaning there'll likely be little excitement and potentially fewer people at the polls. Still, Crystal Zermeno, the director of special projects for the Democratic field organization Texas Organizing Project, said Hispanic voter outreach hasn't been a top priority for decades.

"Very little is spent on the field, going out there and knocking on doors," Zermeno said. "And you have to have real, authentic conversations with people. Simply showing up isn't enough."

A 2014 Gallup poll found that Texas Hispanics prefer Democrats to Republicans by a 19 percentage-point margin. Nationwide, Democrats enjoy a more comfortable 30 percentage-point advantage.

So, the state Republican Party has staffers focused on boosting minority turnout; Ted Cruz became the first Hispanic elected to the U.S. Senate from Texas in 2012, despite his support for strict immigration policies.

Sergio Terreros, a 34-year-old marketing professional in Houston originally from Monterrey, Mexico, who became a U.S. citizen last year, said he may vote for Trump.

"I don't like the hate he talks about," Terreros said. "But I do agree with what he says about running the country like a business."

Terreros was attending the same festival as Villenas, who continued approaching would-be voters despite numerous rejections. Finally, she found Jonathan Avalos waiting in line for free McDonalds smoothies. The 18-year-old agreed to register to vote for the first time, though Avalos said he's not sure he'll actually cast a November ballot.

"I'd heard about Trump and everything," he said. "But I really have no idea what's going on."

Macon, Georgia
Neighbor churches work to heal divide

The racial separation of churches is an enduring embarrassment for many Americans Christians. For decades, they have tried to find ways to come together with little progress beyond occasional pulpit swaps and joint worship.

These two churches in Macon, Georgia, were trying for something deeper and more enduring, an effort that would require courageously confronting a past many preferred to leave unexamined.

Writing this story involved a lot of reading, including a 400-page record of the white church and books on racism in Southern religion. In the interviews with the pastors and church members, it was amazing to see how a history many

Americans consider ancient _ about abolition, the Civil War, Jim Crow and the civil rights movement _ could still play such a strong role in shaping the relationship between these two congregations.

—Rachel Zoll, AP National Religion Writer

* * *

There are two First Baptist Churches in Macon—one black and one white. They sit almost back-to-back, separated by a small park, in a hilltop historic district overlooking downtown.

"We're literally around the corner from each other," said the Rev. Scott Dickison, pastor of the white church.

About 170 years ago, they were one congregation, albeit a church of masters and slaves. Then the fight over abolition and slavery started tearing badly at religious groups and moving the country toward Civil War. The Macon church, like many others at the time, decided it was time to separate by race.

Ever since—through Jim Crow, the civil rights movement, desegregation and beyond—the division endured, becoming so deeply rooted it hardly drew notice. Jarred Moore, whose family has belonged to the black church for three generations, said he didn't know the details of the history until recently.

"I thought, 'First Baptist, First Baptist?' There are two First Baptists right down the street from each other and I always wondered about it," said Moore, a public school teacher.

Then, two years ago, Dickison and the pastor of the black church, the Rev. James Goolsby, met over lunch and an idea took shape: They'd try to find a way the congregations, neighbors for so long, could become friends. They'd try to bridge the stubborn divide of race.

They are taking up this work against a painful and tumultuous backdrop: the massacre last year at a historic black church in Charleston, South Carolina; the much-publicized deaths of blacks at the hands of law enforcement; the rise of the Black Lives Matter movement, and the sniper killing of white Dallas police officers. These events, and the tensions they have raised, have become part of the tentative new discussions among congregants at the two First Baptists.

Next month, the pastors will take their most ambitious step yet, leading joint discussions with church members on racism in the history of the U.S., and also in the history of their congregations.

"This is not a conversation of blame, but of acceptance and moving forward," said Goolsby, sitting in the quiet sanctuary of his church on a Monday morning. "What will govern how quickly we move is when there's a certain level of understanding of the past."

The South is dotted with cities that have two First Baptist Churches.

In the early 19th century, before the Civil War, whites and blacks often worshipped together, sharing faith but not pews; blacks were restricted to galleries or the back of the sanctuary. Eventually, black populations started growing faster in many communities. Whites, made uneasy by the imbalance, responded by splitting up the congregations.

This was apparently the case for First Baptist in Macon.

In 1845, church leaders bought property a block away, as "a place and habitation for the religious service and moral cultivation and improvement of the colored portion" of the congregation, according to the deed. A building was quickly erected and the black church opened.

That was a year when tensions between anti- and pro-slavery Baptists boiled over nationwide, leading Southerners to break away and create their own denomination, the Southern Baptist Convention, which upheld

The First Baptist Church, now a predominantly African-American congregation, in Macon, GA, July 11, 2016. (AP Photo/Branden Camp)

slavery as ordained by God. The white Macon congregation, known as the First Baptist Church of Christ, became Southern Baptist.

Whites maintained oversight of the black church as required by Georgia law at the time for fear of slave rebellions. But after the Civil War ended in 1865, the white church fully severed ties.

The two First Baptist Churches stayed that way, just steps from each other but apart, ever since.

Religious groups try to set a moral standard that rises above the issues and ideologies dividing society. But faith leaders often fall short of that ideal, reflecting or even exacerbating the rifts. Like many other American institutions, houses of worship have largely been separated by race, to the point that the Rev. Martin Luther King Jr. called Sunday mornings "one of the most segregated hours." Recently, more churches have tried to diversify and to look critically at their past actions and teachings, with denominations from the Southern Baptist Convention to the Episcopal Church making a priority of fighting racial bias.

When Goolsby last year told the black church of the plan to work with the white congregation, people applauded. White congregants were enthusiastic as well. Yet, it was excitement mixed with some apprehension, since the effort would inevitably require "some challenging conversations," Dickison said.

"It's hard to talk honestly about race," said Doug Thompson, a member of the white church and also a Mercer University professor who specializes in religion and race. "It's always hard to help people move forward."

The two churches' first activity together was modest but symbolically significant. For years, each church held its Easter egg hunt in the same tree-shaded park behind their churches, but at different times. Last year, they met there together. Photos from the joint gathering show children huddled together for a group picture, grasping pink, blue and yellow baskets, black faces and white faces squinting into the sun.

As the churches held other combined activities—a book drive, a Thanksgiving potluck—some participants were so moved they had tears in their eyes. There were members of both churches who said they had been waiting for decades for such a reunion.

"I thought it would be a great opportunity and a blessing," said Bea Warbington-Ross, a retired human resources specialist and member of

Goolsby's congregation. "There's no reason for Sunday to be the most seg-regated day."

Congregants were surprised to learn their sanctuaries had nearly identical designs, with vaulted ceilings that resembled the inverted hull of a ship. Warbington-Ross lives in the historic district five blocks from the white church, which some of her neighbors attend. She'd never been inside.

While the visits back and forth and the joint activities are clearly establishing connections, the churches are not working toward a merger.

"We don't want to be one congregation again. We want to be a family," said Jessica Northenor, a public school teacher and member of the white church who is helping shape the new relationship.

The congregations sealed their commitment to each other at a joint Pentecost service at the black church. Before a choir drawn from both congregations, leaders pledged to work together under the auspices of the New Baptist Covenant, an organization formed by President Jimmy Carter to unite Baptists.

"If you hold onto the pain of the past, you don't allow God to minister and bless you in the days to come," Goolsby said in his sermon that day. "We can show in our relationship what it means to be a child of God."

But the pastors acknowledge the long journey ahead. They are tackling what some call the original sin of the country's founding. The influence of racial inequity on U.S. history and modern-day life is, of course, a contentious and sensitive issue. Consider reaction to the recent comment by first lady Michelle Obama that slaves built the White House, a reference long acknowledged by historians as fact but one that critics complained was unpatriotic.

In Macon, where plaques and monuments commemorating Confederate soldiers' valor adorn street corners and parks, white congregants will be asked to re-examine their own church history, which until recently had been officially recorded in mostly benign terms. It reflected a perspective of white "good paternalism" toward the black congregation, Thompson said, with almost no recognition of racism.

The review is so sensitive that Goolsby had suggested early on that the two churches wait to address the past until they built more mutual trust and goodwill. Dickison, acknowledging that some congregants will be embarrassed and some distressed or resistant, considers the conversation vital.

"A white person from the South—to not come to terms with our own history and experience with race is to deprive ourselves of a full understanding of the Gospel. We need to go through this kind of conversion experience of confession, of repentance and of reconciliation. We need to have that when it comes to race, not just in the country but within the church," Dickison said.

* * *

Goolsby, a 59-year-old Atlanta native and graduate of Morehouse College and Mercer's McAfee School of Theology, has been pastor at the black church for more than 12 years. He said he and a previous pastor at the white church tried to build ties between the congregations but the effort didn't go very far.

This time is different, he said, in part because of his relationship with Dickison. The 33-year-old North Carolina native and Harvard Divinity School graduate became a pastor in Macon about four years ago. He and Goolsby have attended meetings of Carter's organization, and last month took their families to meet the former president on a Sunday at Carter's church in Plains, Georgia.

"We've already seen the fruits of this," Goolsby said.

He recalled that after the attack last year on the Charleston church, he was in the parking lot of a J.C. Penney store, waiting for his wife, when Dickison called.

"Scott shared how he felt, how he was struggling with what he would share with his congregation," Goolsby said. The two discussed the history of violence against black churches, and Dickison asked how he could show support.

"I said, 'We're already doing it,'" Goolsby said. "The mere fact he thought to call me was huge."

The stakes were even more personal about six months later, when the white church invited black church members for a youth trip to Orlando.

Goolsby's teenage son was among those invited. But Goolsby had considered Florida a danger ever since Trayvon Martin, an unarmed, black 17-year-old, was fatally shot in Sanford by George Zimmerman, a neighborhood watch volunteer who was later acquitted of second-degree murder and manslaughter charges.

The First Baptist Church of Christ, a predominantly white congregation, in Macon, GA, July 10, 2016. (AP Photo/Branden Camp)

The pastor could not let his son go on the trip. "If you put a hoodie on him," he said, "he looks just like Trayvon."

The concerns of anxious black parents had been much in the news amid the shootings of black men. But the white church members hadn't had to confront the issue directly until Goolsby raised it.

"It's one thing to understand it intellectually and another thing to understand it emotionally. Once he said that, I could feel it," said David Cooke, a white deacon, who is also the Macon-Bibb County district attorney.

Cooke was to be a chaperone on the Orlando trip. He promised Goolsby he would be especially watchful. The trip went ahead safely with young people from both congregations—including the pastor's son.

"The fact that that was so easy to share—we've already made progress," Goolsby said.

Dickison strode into the basement hall of his church with a box under one arm. Inside, were copies of "Strength to Love," a collection of sermons and writings by King. The book was at the center of classes that Dickison organized on racism for the white church, in preparation for the talks next month.

But the readings had extra significance that morning. It was the Sunday after the fatal police shootings of Alton Sterling in Louisiana and Philando Castile in Minnesota, and the fatal ambush on Dallas police. "It's weeks like these when we need more than ever to be with God's people," Dickison told the roomful of congregants.

With the stifling humidity of a Georgia summer building outside, he launched into a discussion of King's sermon on the parable of the Good Samaritan, about despised groups and showing mercy.

"We have our tribes. We see ourselves over and against others," he said, then asked church members to reflect.

One man said when you reach out to someone from another group, "you're perceived as unpatriotic," or disloyal.

A woman said fear often kept people from crossing racial divides. "What if you make it worse?" she asked.

Another woman said she was upset to see some disrespect of the police. She compared law enforcement officers to the Good Samaritan, who helped a wounded stranger others had ignored. "They rush toward danger when others run," she said.

Dickison acknowledged "fear is powerful" in shaping reactions to others. After more discussion, he wrapped up the session by quoting King, who said the solution to racism is the "willingness of men to obey the unenforceable."

"We can't survive spiritually separate," the white pastor said.

That same morning, at the service at the black church, the congregation announced it would host the city's Black Lives Matter vigil, marking the tragedies of the preceding week.

The movement has been a topic at meetings of a group appointed by Goolsby and Dickison, comprised of representatives of each church, to help guide their new relationship.

"I think it's an opportunity for healing," said Warbington-Ross, who is part of the group. "It's an opportunity for us to just inform the church that black lives matter also as it relates to inclusion and exclusion, and to inform them of some things that they take for granted that we have to endure, like racial profiling, like police brutality, like racial inequality, those kinds of things."

At the vigil the next night, police officers directed traffic as people climbed the steep marble church steps, where "God's Mighty Fortress" is engraved in gold. Clergy from across the city filled one side of the broad pulpit. Cooke, the prosecutor, and the county sheriff were among those representing law enforcement; community leaders and residents nearly filled the pews.

A speaker wearing a Black Lives Matter T-shirt explained the movement "was not birthed out of hate. It was birthed out of hurt."

Goolsby and Dickison sat side-by-side on the pulpit, swaying along with the hymns, then stood together to speak. Dickison compared racism to "a cancer that roams inside the body of this nation, and yes, even in the body of Christ." Goolsby urged people to maintain hope "in spite of our circumstances," and he added, "We know there will be change."

Said both men: "Amen."

Waukegan, Illinois
In recovery, many poor schools left behind

We chose to base this story about the wide disparity in school funding at two school districts in suburban Chicago for several reasons: We knew from crunching the data that Illinois is one of the least equitable states when it comes to the amount of money spent per student and the gap between "rich" and "poor" districts. Stevenson and Waukegan are only 20 miles apart, making for a good journalistic comparison, and they were easily accessible from our bureaus in Chicago and Milwaukee, where our team was based. They also were two of the only Illinois districts still in session when we launched this project in mid-May.

As striking as the contrast is between these districts, readers should know that there are many, many districts in Illinois (and across the U.S.) that are far poorer than Waukegan. A few weeks before we started this project I traveled about six hours south of Chicago to Harrisburg, Illinois, a speck of a town that has been hit hard by the decline in the coal industry. There, and at other rural districts in the area, I toured schools and held textbooks so old they were literally falling apart. I talked to students worried that if state lawmakers didn't approve an education budget their schools would close, because their districts had almost no cash reserves. I met a superintendent who had to choose between fixing a boiler or laying off teachers (she opted to keep the heat on). The one constant was the passion of the people who work in our schools, wherever they are. At Stevenson High School, there was a bubbly young teacher who was more excited than anyone I have ever seen about — of all things — physics. In Harrisburg, there's a superintendent who's fighting like hell for the kids in his district, taking his tough talk to town halls and the state Capitol. At an elementary school in Waukegan, special education teacher Michelle Lenczuk ducked out of a stifling classroom to chat with us in a stairwell. She said she'd gotten job offers from wealthier districts but had chosen to stay where she is, teaching children whose families struggle to get by, because she loves the kids and their parents so much.

When she finished talking, Lenczuk looked down at her arms and told us that she had goosebumps. We did too.

—Sara Burnett, AP Reporter

* * *

Consider Waukegan and Stevenson, two Illinois school districts separated by 20 miles — and an enormous financial gulf.

Stevenson, mostly white, is flush with resources. The high school has five different spaces for theater performances, two gyms, an Olympic-size pool and an espresso bar.

Meanwhile Waukegan, with its mostly minority student body, is struggling. At one school, the band is forced to practice in a hallway, and as many as 28 students share a single computer.

Last year, Stevenson spent close to $18,800 per student. Waukegan's expenditure? About $12,600.

And the gap has only been getting wider — here in the suburbs north of Chicago, and in many places across the nation. In the years following the 2008 financial crisis, school districts serving poor communities generally have been hit harder than more affluent districts, according to an Associated Press analysis of local, state and federal education spending.

The result has been a worsening of America's rich schools, poor schools divide—and its racial divide, because many poor districts are also heavily minority. It also perpetuates the perception that the system is rigged in favor of the haves, at the expense of the have-nots—a major driver of America's angst in this election year.

The AP found that aid to local districts from the federal government surged after the economic downturn, as part of the stimulus, but then receded. Schools were left to rely more on state funding that has not bounced back to pre-recession levels. And poorer districts that cannot draw on healthy property tax bases have been left in the lurch.

The effects vary widely across the 50 states. Each has its own unique funding formula.

For example, per-pupil spending in poorer Missouri districts fell behind richer districts in 2013—the first time in a well over decade.

Most rich districts have seen a steady increase in revenue while poorer districts—such as Louisiana RII, a predominantly white district 80 miles northwest of St. Louis—have seen cuts since 2010. That rural district has started waiting longer to replace textbooks, and it will likely abandon initiatives to distribute new computers and to bring wireless internet into classrooms. Todd Smith, the superintendent, said the district will likely seek a tax increase or a bond sale because there isn't enough money for basic maintenance.

"We find ourselves more and more dipping into our reserves," Smith said.

In Connecticut's largest city, Bridgeport, schools have struggled with cuts in state and federal grants, Superintendent Frances Rabinowitz said. And the gap widens between her district and neighboring, affluent Fairfield County towns with smaller class sizes and students with far fewer needs.

The result? No aides for kindergarten classrooms, or guidance counselors for elementary schools, or buses for students at some high schools (they get city bus passes, instead).

"I feel like I am cutting the lifeblood of the system," said Rabinowitz, whose schools are more than 80 percent black or Hispanic. "We're not

Students gather between classes in a lounge area overlooking an Olympic-size pool at Stevenson High School in Lincolnshire, IL, May 24, 2016. (AP Photo/Nam Y. Huh)

talking nice things. We're talking what I would consider essentials in trying to move the district forward."

The impact can be long-lasting, researchers say. A study for the non-profit and non-partisan National Bureau of Economic Research tracked students enrolled in districts where there was a prolonged increase in school funding.

Students educated in flush times finished more years of school, were less likely to live in poverty as adults, and made about 7.25 percent more in wages.

"The body of evidence is pretty clear that when school districts get more money, good things tend to happen and when they're forced to cut spending, bad things tend to happen," said Kirabo Jackson, one of the report's authors and an associate professor of human development and social policy at Northwestern University's School of Education and Social Policy.

The widening funding gap that favors richer schools in Illinois is an extreme example.

For schools in the poorest 25 percent of Illinois districts, as measured by child poverty rates, per-pupil funding stalled at around $13,500 in 2014, the most recent year for which full data are available. Meanwhile, per-pupil funding climbed to over $15,000 in the wealthiest 25 percent.

Alejandra Ocampo, last year's senior class president at Waukegan High School, said the disparities are plain to see.

When her athletic teams would travel to other schools for competitions, the affluence was clear from the minute they pulled up, Ocampo says. And sometimes when those opposing teams would show up to Waukegan, they would hear the chatter: "This is it?" or "Why is their locker room like a dungeon?"

Waukegan District 60's enrollment of roughly 17,000 is nearly 80 percent Hispanic and 15 percent black students, and includes a higher-than-average percentage of English language learners and children in poverty. The district struggled to meet the needs of its students even before the foreclosure crisis left blocks dotted with empty homes and businesses. Teachers buy fans with their own money to fight the heat at schools like the district's Little Fort Elementary.

Over the past five years, the district lost $43 million in state aid because Illinois cut education funding, according to Gwendolyn Polk, associate superintendent of business and financial services. The proposed budget for

Students eat lunch inside the school's gym at Little Fort Elementary School in Waukegan, IL, June 7, 2016. (AP Photo/Kamil Krzaczynski)

the coming year is $218 million, with a projected deficit of $7.4 million. The district did its best to keep the cuts from affecting the classroom, which meant putting off regular maintenance and cobbling together funds to deal with emergencies.

When a water pipe began leaking in a classroom, the district was required to remove asbestos around the aged pipes as part of the repairs. Workers ripped open a 6-foot hole, then covered it with a piece of plywood and painted over it.

About 70 percent of students graduate from Waukegan High School in four years, and less than half go on to attend a two-year or four-year college.

"Just because our students are low income here within this district, it doesn't mean they shouldn't have the same opportunities kids in surrounding districts have," said Michelle Lenczuk, a teacher at Little Fort. "They have the same knowledge. They have the same capability to learn. They have the drive. They want to do that."

Stevenson District 125, in contrast, educates students in an area northwest of Chicago that's home to upper-class professionals and corporate headquarters, the kind of districts parents move into in hopes of giving their children a leg up. Adlai Stevenson High School resembles a small college, with a manicured campus and more than 120 student clubs. Wide, carpeted hallways house art galleries for displaying student work. Outside a suite of teacher offices, a message on a flat-screen TV congratulates the water polo team on its state championship.

Two-thirds of the students are white and about 22 percent are Asian, with black and Hispanic students making up less than 10 percent of the enrollment. Between 97 and 98 percent of students will go on to college, most of them to four-year schools.

Stevenson has felt minimal impact from state budget cuts, spokesman Jim Conrey said. The district hasn't had to go to referendum to get more property tax revenue since 2002, when a measure passed with 70 percent support.

"We're certainly well aware of what other schools are suffering through right now and we sympathize with them," Conrey said. "We're very lucky in that we're not having to face a lot of the issues that they are."

Matthew Cabrera, a 17-year-old who just finished his junior year at Stevenson, takes a range of Advanced Placement classes and plays violin in the school orchestra. His family moved to the area from the South Side of Chicago when Cabrera was in second grade, and he knows how different Stevenson is from the school he would have attended if they'd stayed.

"I don't think I would have been able to grow as a person as much if I didn't go to Stevenson," Cabrera says.

Waukegan's Alejandra Ocampo plans to study education and Spanish in college this fall. She's proud of where she comes from, but she says some more money would be helpful in ways that go beyond better facilities or more teachers.

"I feel like funding is more of a motivational gift than an actual physical gift," she said. "It's how it makes you feel about yourself."

Hannibal, Ohio

How China fueled pain and Trump support

My parents are from the coal fields of West Virginia. So it's been painful for me to watch the region's economic decline. This Divided America story gave me a chance to visit Appalachia and talk to those who have been displaced by forces beyond their control.

I write about international economics, a beat that for the past couple of years has included monitoring the fallout from China's steady economic slowdown. The Chinese economy is fascinating, but its travails can seem a little abstract for American readers.

At a hearing of the U.S.-China Economic and Security Commission in February, I came across some stunning numbers that showed how what happens in China doesn't necessarily stay in China: The data, compiled by the U.S. Geological Survey, documented how China has flooded the world with aluminum, driving the price of the metal into the ground. I wondered how whether China's over-production was hurting U.S. aluminum producers. A quick search showed that it was: U.S. aluminum companies were closing or idling smelters across the country. I zeroed in on the closing of a plant in Hannibal, Ohio, which had drawn a lot of workers from neighboring West Virginia.

Around the same time, I came across a study by economist David Autor of MIT (and others), showing that people in communities that had been hit hard by Chinese competition tended to reject mainstream politicians and go for "strident" alternatives. Sure enough, the results of the Ohio Republican primary showed that folks around the closed Hannibal plant were embracing Donald Trump (and rejecting native son John Kasich). So I thought we had a compelling way to look at the way global economic forces hurt a specific American community and aided Trump's campaign.

— **Paul Wiseman, AP Economics Reporter**

* * *

Crushed by Chinese competition and feeling betrayed by mainstream politicians, workers in the hills of eastern Ohio are embracing Donald Trump and his tough talk on trade.

For decades, they and others living across the Ohio River in West Virginia found work in coal mines and at a local aluminum plant—union jobs, with good pay and generous benefits.

But those jobs are going, if not gone.

Coal is being wiped out by stricter environmental rules and competition from cheap natural gas. The Ormet aluminum plant? It's out of business, doomed by China's domination of the global aluminum market.

In an angry election year, some of America's angriest voters live in places like Monroe County where local economies have been punished by price competition with China. Their frustration has fueled support for the Republican presidential nominee, with his belligerent rhetoric about the need to outsmart America's economic rivals, tear up unfair trade deals and re-establish America as the world's dominant player.

"This is Trump country," says John Saunders, an official with the United Steelworkers in nearby Martins Ferry, Ohio.

The disaster that's unfolded here isn't obvious at first glance, not in a region known as the Switzerland of Ohio for its forested, rolling hills. In tiny Hannibal (population: 411), stately two-story homes overlook lawns that roll toward the banks of the Ohio. Nearby Woodsfield, seat of Monroe County, Ohio, looks like Main Street USA, its downtown dominated by a red brick courthouse displaying one of the world's biggest clocks.

But the misery is real. Monroe County's unemployment rate is Ohio's highest at 10.2 percent. Families have moved out to find work. The number of children in the local school district is down 223, or nearly 10 percent, since 2013.

A diesel tank at the former Ormet plant in Hannibal, Ohio. For decades, the plant was a major employer in the area, but it closed in 2014, crushed by Chinese competition. (AP Photo/Paul Vernon)

"You're going to have to travel to find a job," says Fran Poole, whose husband, Cecil, worked at the Ormet plant here for 37 years before being laid off when it closed.

Some laid-off workers chose to retire early. Others found work in the energy business, only to see those jobs melt away, too, as oil and gas prices fell. Some are doing odd jobs—cutting grass, hauling gravel.

Much of the damage to this region can be traced to China's decision to become self-sufficient in aluminum production. Aluminum is used in construction and auto manufacturing, aerospace and consumer-product packaging. The surge in its production reflected a broader Chinese strategy: pour money into manufacturing to add jobs and accelerate economic growth.

Fueled by government subsidies and cheap loans from state-owned banks, Chinese aluminum producers went into overdrive: In 2000, the United States had produced a world-beating 15 percent of all aluminum, China just 11 percent. By 2015, China had escalated its output nearly 1,200 percent—and held 55 percent of the world's share.

As Chinese aluminum flooded the world, prices collapsed. A pound of raw aluminum now fetches 74 cents—down from $1.25 five years ago. U.S. production has tumbled 56 percent since 2000, according to the U.S. Geological Survey. And America's share of world aluminum is below 3 percent.

Since 2011, U.S. aluminum companies have closed or idled nine of the 14 U.S. smelters, where aluminum oxide is turned into raw aluminum. Two surviving plants are running at half capacity or less. In Massena, New York; Columbia Falls, Montana; New Madrid, Missouri, plants have folded, idled production or laid off workers.

Hundreds of workers in New Madrid lost their jobs when Noranda Aluminum Holding Corp. sought bankruptcy protection in February.

"If you take metal prices back to where they were before China started flooding the market, you're looking at somewhere between 90 cents and $1.10 a pound," says Cameron Redd, a laid-off Noranda employee. At those prices, he says, the Noranda plant still "would be hiring."

Relief hasn't come. At this month's G-20 summit, U.S. and Chinese officials agreed to work together to reduce overproduction of aluminum, but the Chinese have long balked at cutting aluminum output—and jobs.

"They don't want unemployment," says Michael Komesaroff of Urandaline Investments, and Australian consulting firm.

Longtime residents recall how vital the Ormet plant here was for the area's economy and for supporting middle-class lifestyles. Workers regularly vacationed and bought houses and boats and all-terrain vehicles to tear up the Ohio countryside.

"If you didn't go to college or the military, you went to the coal mines or Ormet," says Bill Long, a former Ormet laborer who is a supervisor at the county's Department of Job and Family Services.

The plant used to burn more electricity than all of Pittsburgh. For nearly six decades, barges plied the Ohio River and trains clacked alongside State Highway 7, bearing Ormet aluminum to customers across America.

The factory drew workers from the hills of West Virginia and eastern Ohio, paying them about $40,000 a year before overtime. Overtime was "sporadic," recalls Carl Davis, a former Ormet worker who is now a Monroe County commissioner. "But a few were known to gross around $100,000."

"Even though the work was hard back then, it was best job I had ever had, and the most money I'd ever had my hands on," says Francis Blackstone, a 70-year-old Ormet retiree. "And the benefits were just unheard of"—including free health care.

"We were all family," says Danny Isaly, an Ormet worker who became the plant's head of industrial relations. "Everybody had a relative here."

After the plant closed, Isaly received unemployment benefits until they ran out. Then he retired at age 59.

Niagara Worldwide bought the 1,600-acre complex at auction in 2014 after Ormet Corp. sought bankruptcy protection. Dan Gerovac is overseeing the plant's destruction for Niagara. He and his crew are clearing the site in hopes of selling it to another industrial company. They are breaking down equipment—including the pots where aluminum oxide was turned into aluminum at temperatures of 1,800 degrees Fahrenheit—for sale as scrap metal.

"No aluminum will be made here anymore," Gerovac says.

Through most of the 2000s—aside from a sharp drop during the Great Recession—world aluminum prices had withstood the surge in supply from China. China's own economy was growing so fast its demand for aluminum was nearly insatiable. Then its economy decelerated after 2010, and aluminum prices plunged.

Desperate, Ormet and the Steelworkers union sought to renegotiate electricity prices from the local utility, AEP Ohio. In 2012 and 2013, they urged Gov. John Kasich to lean on the state utility commission to help. Kasich wouldn't intervene, leaving the decision to the commission.

The plant went out of business.

Aluminum prices were so low the plant might not have survived anyway. But Kasich's refusal to intervene helps explain why animosity for the governor runs high in these parts. In the March Republican presidential primary, Monroe County overwhelmingly backed Trump and rejected Kasich, who otherwise won his home state handily.

"He just shunned us," Danny Isaly says.

Trump is viewed as a champion to many here who say America's political leaders have stood by while competition from China and other countries has wrecked communities like Hannibal.

Cecil Poole, a former Ormet employee who became a truck driver after he lost his job. As a truck driver, he earned about what he made at Ormet, though he had to work twice as many hours for it. He retired in June, 2016. (AP Photo/Paul Vernon)

"He says what a lot of people would like to say," says Cecil Poole, who feels the national Democratic Party has abandoned blue-collar workers. Trump's pledge to "Make America Great Again" resonates with those who feel they've lost their place in the middle class.

In a way, some of the laid-off Ormet workers were fortunate for a time. When the plant closed two years ago, the region was enjoying an energy boom. Oil and gas companies were fracking in the Marcellus Shale formation, from upstate New York through Pennsylvania, Maryland, Ohio and West Virginia. They needed drivers, electricians, welders.

Poole, 62, and out of work after nearly four decades at Ormet, got a commercial driver's license and found work hauling supplies for energy companies. He earned about what he made at Ormet, though he had to work twice as many hours for it. And Poole found the work exhausting. He traveled overnight and slept in his rig.

"It was tough on the old body," he says.

He retired in June.

The fracking boom, it turned out, didn't produce as many jobs as people here had hoped. The energy companies often brought in experienced oil-field workers. Then, energy prices started tumbling, and fracking work dried up.

Now, job openings are scarce, the pay and benefits no match for what Ormet offered.

"It's embarrassing what's out there," says Bill Long, who counsels the unemployed.

Peeking out from one jobseeker's file in his office is an application for a position at Dairy Queen. Long says some of the old Ormet workers seem in denial about their prospects. He recently ran into one.

"He said, 'I keep hoping the plant's going to fire back up,'" Long recalls. "I said, 'That's not going to happen, buddy.'"

Kansas City, Missouri
Minorities hopeful, whites sour on future

As a political reporter you spend a lot of time talking to strangers. In the tony suburb of Leawood, Kansas I found Carole Ramsey loading up her Lexus SUV and asked her about the election. She was frank about the amazingly fortunate life she'd led, the affluent retirement she and her husband enjoy and the fears that her grandkids won't be able to enjoy that. She embodied much of the anxiety you hear from white voters during the election — poor or wealthy, pro-Trump or against him.

The next day I had one of those you-can't-make-it-up moments as a reporter. I was in a beauty salon in a proud, yet poor, Kansas City neighborhood and Ethel Tuggle began to complain about how her grandkids have life almost too easy — pulling in

$15, $20 an hour, not having to see the rank racism she dealt with growing up as a black girl in midcentury Missouri. She walked slowly into the rideshare van that carried her away to her nearby home, a symbol of the hope and optimism that minorities still have nowadays.

To me that's the story of this election and the politics of this century so far. Whites are worried that the country's best days are behind it as they lose their privileged position in American society. Minorities, seeing doors open up for them and their numbers growing, are feeling more and more hopeful. It explains the radical difference in tone between the two parties, why conservative populism has so far been unable to make inroads among poor minority communities. And it explains so many of the random conversations I've had as a reporter over the past decade with anxious whites compared to the relative calm with which both black and Latino voters have greeted the crazy twists and turns of the 21st century.

—Nicholas Riccardi, AP Western Political Writer

* * *

Consider two women in their 70s, both residents of the Kansas City area. One is white and affluent; the other is black and working class. Guess which one is more optimistic about the country's future and that of their grandchildren? More than likely, you guessed wrong.

This year's presidential campaign has underscored an economic paradox: Financially, black Americans and Hispanics are far worse off than whites, yet polls show minorities are more likely than whites to believe in the American Dream. And they are less anxious about the outcome of the election.

At 71, Carole Ramsey knows she has long been fortunate. She married a man who became a successful lawyer, raised their children in Kansas City's affluent western suburbs and now enjoys a comfortable retirement full of international travel. "We've lived a very good life," Ramsey, who is white, said at an upscale shopping center in Leawood, Kansas. Even so, she says she'll vote for Donald Trump because she fears economic stagnation and global terrorism. "Our kids will not be able to live the way we did, that's for sure."

Ethel Tuggle, 72, backs Hillary Clinton, and a big reason is that her grandchildren's circumstances show how life has improved for her family.

"They're starting jobs at $15, $20 an hour; I've never seen that sort of money," said Tuggle, who is black and worked construction for Kansas City government until injuries forced her to retire early. Tuggle says she's amazed at the progress she's witnessed since her childhood in rural Missouri, when she was barred from entering shoe stores and had to trace her foot on a sheet of paper so a salesman inside could fit her for shoes. Her grandchildren live under the nation's first black president.

One factor in the surprising gap between black optimism and white pessimism is simply partisan politics: Blacks and Hispanics are overwhelmingly Democrats and more likely to feel positive about the future when one of their own is in the White House. "When Bush was in office, Republicans thought the country was headed in the right direction," while Democrats did not, said Neil Newhouse, a Republican pollster. "Once Democrats took over, that flipped." Still, there's evidence that the divide goes beyond party and Obama's presidency. In great measure, it has to do with the past, not the future: Minorities who have seen great improvements in their lives are more confident, while whites who have seen disintegration in their lives are more pessimistic.

The NORC at the University of Chicago has for decades asked Americans whether they think their standard of living will improve. Since 2002—well before Obama's 2008 election—NORC surveys have found that whites across all parties and income levels have been steadily less likely to think their standard of living would improve. Blacks and Hispanics, meanwhile, have increasingly believed their living standards would rise. "This is a racial and ethnic thing—not something that's based on education, income or party," said Jennifer Benz of NORC. "It's whites' huge decline in optimism that makes the gap between whites and minorities the biggest it's been in a long time."

In a poll conducted for the Atlantic and Aspen Institute last year, minorities were more likely than whites to agree with the statement, "The American Dream is alive and well."

A Pew Foundation survey found that Hispanics were the least likely ethnic or racial group to be anxious about the outcome of the current presidential race—even though a centerpiece of Trump's platform is to deport millions of immigrants living in the country illegally and restrict overall immigration.

In a June AP-NORC poll, 62 percent of blacks said they thought America's best days were ahead. Only 40 percent of whites thought so. Fifty-three percent of blacks and 48 percent of Hispanics called the economy "good." Just 37 percent of whites did.

The level of optimism among minorities might seem to defy economic realities. Whites have a median household income of $71,300 compared with blacks' median of $43,300. A Pew foundation report found that white households' typical net worth was 13 times that of black households. A separate report from the Institute for Policy Studies has calculated that, at their current rate, it would take blacks 228 years to catch up with the wealth of whites.

Still, minorities have seen progress, while whites have stalled.

According to Census data, white men have increased their income by only 3 percent since 1973, while black men have improved theirs by 12 percent. (Incomes for all women have risen sharply since they entered and rose through the workforce since the early 1970s.) Many Hispanics have enjoyed solid income gains. The Institute for Policy Studies found that Hispanics' household wealth has risen 69 percent over the past 30 years, albeit to a still-low $98,000 relative to whites' $656,000. "If you're at the bottom moving up, you feel much better about your prospects than if you're at the top moving down," Democratic pollster Mark Mellman said.

There is one area where blacks, especially, register as more pessimistic than whites: Race relations and policing. Blacks particularly have polled as more negative about race relations recently, following a series of high-profile police killings of African-Americans. There is frustration, especially among younger blacks, that the incidents have continued under the nation's first African-American president. Yet even the usually peaceful demonstrations against those killings since 2014 could be seen as evidence of optimism, said Andra Gillespie, a political scientist at Atlanta's Emory University. "You wouldn't see people taking to the streets and demanding justice if they didn't think they had a greater chance of being able to change things," Gillespie said.

Brandon Dixon's father was asphyxiated by Kansas City police in 2009 during a psychotic episode. The incident shocked Dixon, who gave up his work in construction and decided to plow his family's life's savings into opening a restaurant in the impoverished neighborhood where he grew up.

Brandon Dixon stands in the restaurant he is trying to open in Kansas City, MO, September 6, 2016. (AP Photo/Charlie Riedel)

Four years after he bought a former beauty salon to convert into an eatery, Dixon has been unable to open the restaurant because of environmental contamination from a neighboring gas station. He's struggling financially but hopes his business will finally open in a few weeks, and that it will help turn around his life and his community. "We've always seen adversity," Dixon said. "You have to not stand still, not be stagnating, keep moving forward."

Andrew Cherlin, a sociologist at Johns Hopkins University, noted that people tend to evaluate their own prospects based on their parents' experiences. "When whites look backwards, they compare themselves to a generation that was doing better," Cherlin said. "Blacks and Hispanics," who face less overt discrimination today, "compare themselves to a generation that was doing worse."

As incomes have stagnated for working class whites, their rates of suicide, drug addiction and mortality have surged. Two economists in December 2015 reported that death rates have been rising since 1999 for whites between ages 45 and 54, with the sharpest increase among the least educated. By contrast, the suicide rate for black men has dropped since 1999. And the gap between black and white life expectancy is now the lowest in more than a century: 3.4 years. More whites have died than were born since 2011, and the Census Bureau projects that whites will be in the minority by 2060.

Doug Haag lives in Milwaukee. One of the city's dwindling number of working-class white residents, he feels that the social contract between employers and employees has broken down. Haag, 59, doesn't see much job security anymore. He works for the state of Wisconsin, where a recent civil service overhaul makes it easier to fire public employees. Even though he's had a steady job the past 18 years he considers himself "lower-middle class," unable to afford vacations or nights out with friends. He worries about whether he'll be able to retire. "There's no middle class any more—the true middle class," Haag said. "There's no loyalty from companies any more or from the employees." A Trump supporter, Haag said he's hopeful that the reality show star can restore the country's position of strength in the world and in the economy. "He's going to be able to do that as a businessman," Haag said.

Adrianne Bockhorst with her 4-year-old daughter, Isla, in the backyard of their home in Whitefish Bay, WI, August. 2, 2016. (AP Photo/Scott Bauer)

Adrianne Bockhorst lives in a tonier spot than Haag—in the upscale Milwaukee suburb of Whitefish Bay. She's a Democrat who plans to vote for Hillary Clinton. But she, too, is worried—shaken by the scars of the recession, which tossed her family into bankruptcy, and by the vitriol of the presidential campaign. Bockhorst, who is white, tries not to even think of the country's economic future. "I just ignore it because it scares me so much because of the collapse and what it did to us, our dreams," she said. "I'm in total denial that something bad could happen again. We don't have a retirement plan, we don't have a safety net." Bockhorst lives worlds away from the Milwaukee streets which erupted in riots last month in the wake of the shooting of a 23-year-old black man by police after a traffic stop. Milwaukee has the fifth-worst poverty rate in the nation, based on the most recent Census data. But even there you'll find optimism among minorities.

"We used to have slaves, you know?" said Christine Ricks, whose northside neighborhood was at the center of August's riots. "There have been improvements. My grandfather and your grandfather used to not be

Substitute teacher Christine Ricks talks about the volunteer work she does to help inner city kids in Milwaukee and how she's optimistic her financial life will improve, August 2, 2016 (AP Photo/Scott Bauer)

able to drink out of the same fountain." Ricks grew up next to what Ricks calls "the biggest dope house in the entire city"; she works as a substitute teacher and has almost no money. But she's still optimistic that her life will improve, and that Clinton will be elected. "I think it's going to be all right; I just don't know how," Ricks said. "I would describe it as complete faith in God. Literally. From moment to moment."

Jose Estrada, 71, emigrated from Mexico to California in the 1960s. He moved to Milwaukee in 1967, became a citizen 11 years later, and retired in 2003 after working a variety of manufacturing jobs. Estrada describes himself as middle class. "I worked very, very hard to get myself to this point," he said. While he supports Clinton and fears Trump would damage the country, Estrada is optimistic about America's future regardless. "We will be happy with anyone who gets into that position, and I will respect it," Estrada said. "Whoever it is, I am living in this country, it is a beautiful country and I love it. I've got more here than I ever had in Mexico."

....

San Francisco, CA
Divided on flag, anthem, other symbols

by Janie Har, AP Reporter

The oldest Latino civil rights group in the United States opens every meeting with the Pledge of Allegiance, a tradition resulting from a long fight to prove Hispanics belong in this country.

In the San Francisco Bay Area, a white father of two says he would never require his young daughters to recite the pledge to show their patriotism.

And in North Dakota, Native American protesters whose ancestors were here long before there was a United States waved American flags as they fought a proposed pipeline near sacred tribal land. Some demonstrators flew the flag upside down as a distress symbol.

San Francisco 49ers quarterback Colin Kaepernick's refusal to stand during "The Star-Spangled Banner" in protest against racial oppression and police brutality has brought to light deep and sometimes surprising differences in the way Americans view the flag, the national anthem and the pledge.

The symbols, people say, inspire skepticism and heartbreak, pride and joy, sometimes all at once in the same person. Some minorities, in particular, have conflicted feelings about symbols honoring a country that has not always treated all people equally.

"The flag is important to us because we have so many relatives in the military," said Justin Poor Bear, a 38-year-old member of the Oglala Lakota tribe from Allen, South Dakota. "There is also a lot of pain."

Following Kaepernick's example, pro athletes and high school students across the country are taking a knee or linking arms during the national anthem before sporting events.

The protests have raised questions of who gets to be called a patriot.

Jason Pontius, a 46-year-old white resident of Alameda, California, said the U.S. of all countries should realize that blind devotion is not the American way. Sometimes when he drops off his second-grader at school, he sticks around while she recites the Pledge of Allegiance with her class. But he doesn't join in.

"What makes America great," he said, "is that people have always challenged the idea of what America stands for."

Yet there are organizations that embrace the flag precisely as a way to declare that their members, too, are Americans.

The League of United Latin American Citizens — the nation's oldest Latino civil rights group, founded in Texas by World War I veterans — has historically opened all its meetings with the pledge and a prayer similar to one George Washington is said to have recited.

Dennis W. Montoya, the league's state director in New Mexico, said the group's emphasis on American pride is connected with a long fight by Latinos to prove they belong in this country.

"If someone doesn't stand for the pledge at one of our meetings, that person will probably be kicked out," Montoya said. "It's disrespecting LULAC's rituals and traditions."

African-Americans have been moved to create symbols that better reflect their history.

The national anthem, for example, was written by a slave owner and contains a painful reference to slavery in its little-known third stanza. The NAACP dubbed "Lift Ev'ry Voice and Sing" the black national anthem in 1919.

The hymn is a staple of African American singers and is so important that the clergy member who gave the benediction at President Barack Obama's 2009 inauguration opened with lines from the song.

After Kaepernick started his protest in August, C.C. Washington of Waco, Texas, read all the stanzas of "The Star-Spangled Banner," including the one that refers derisively to slaves who fought for the British in exchange for their freedom.

The 65-year-old African-American retiree — fresh off visiting the Statue of Liberty last week — felt betrayed.

"All this time, I've been posting on Facebook: Respect our flag, respect our national anthem. Now it's totally different," she said, choking up. "I'll stand out of respect for the people standing next to me, not because I believe it."

Poor Bear said he started looking at the anthem differently after he took a group of Oglala Lakota students to a minor-league hockey game last year. A man yelled slurs and sprayed the children with beer, incensed that one of them did not stand for the national anthem, Poor Bear said. The student had been putting batteries into a camera.

"So I still stand for the national anthem," Poor Bear said. "But I no longer put my hand over my heart."

Linda Tamura, a retired professor of education in Portland, Oregon, has no personal objections to the anthem or the flag, even though her family was among tens of thousands of Japanese-Americans put in internment camps by the U.S. government during World War II.

Her father volunteered for the military, along with her uncle and other Japanese-American men who felt it was their duty. When she looks at the Stars and Stripes, she says, she feels pride, instilled in part by her parents, who "more than anything wanted us to believe in our country."

At the same time, she salutes the growing protest movement and hopes it triggers broader discussions about how to improve relations.

"That's why my father was in the military. That's why we're part of America. That's why we believe in America," she said.

"Because we have the right to say what we believe."

Raleigh, North Carolina
The evolving face of US immigration

A few years ago, a family friend expressed disgust to me about the "Mexicans" moving to his community.

But many of the people moving into his suburb were from India, I responded.

"Same thing," the family friend replied.

The current story about U.S. immigration diverges from the debate in the 2016 presidential election about border walls and the largely Hispanic immigrant population living without visas. Since 2010, immigrants are more likely to hold advanced degrees and arrive from Asia, making them valuable contributors to companies, neighborhoods and the broader U.S. economy. The data were unmistakably clear.

But almost none of this transformation regarding who is coming to America was reflected in remarks by Republican nominee Donald Trump, who has at various points expressed a desire to limit overall immigration levels in the United States. Nor was it fully addressed by Democrat Hillary Clinton.

Instead, the diverse group of foreigners who chose to live in the United States get lumped together in the generic term "immigrant." It would be simple to assume that the U.S. government should only encourage migration by the best and brightest, but through reporting this story the benefits created by the prior wave of Mexican immigrants, even those without visas, pulled into sharper focus. They had repopulated rural farming communities in parts of the country that had been stagnating for decades, generating growth through their daily spending at local stores.

After discussions with Associated Press editors, we decided to anchor this story in North Carolina, where the divide over immigration is among the sharpest in the nation. Parts of the Tarheel State such as Raleigh, Durham and Chapel Hill, the Research Triangle, have thrived in large part because of Indian immigrants who work in tech and the life sciences. But just an hour south of this burgeoning wealth were vast tobacco farms and slaughterhouses where many of the Hispanic immigrants worked, even though the state government had taken steps to crackdown on illegal immigration.

—Josh Boak, AP Economics Writer

* * *

When Manasi Gopala immigrated to America, she finally got the chance to row crew.

As a child in India, she had dreamed of the sport from watching Olympic telecasts. Now, twice a week, she pulls a pair of oars as her scull glides along tree-lined Lake Wheeler, far from her birthplace of Bangalore.

Gopala is among throngs of educated Indians who have moved in recent years to North Carolina's tech-laden Research Triangle and other areas across America. A 39-year-old software developer, she peppers her emails with an adopted "y'all." She became a U.S. citizen three years ago.

"America had given me the opportunity to pursue my own life," she said.

Increasingly, the face of U.S. immigration resembles Gopala.

For all of Donald Trump's talk of building a border wall and deporting 11 million unauthorized immigrants who are mainly Hispanic—and for all

Border Patrol agents look over the primary fence separating Tijuana, Mexico, right, and San Diego in San Diego, June 22, 2016. (AP Photo/Gregory Bull)

of the enduring contention over illegal immigration—immigrants to the U.S. are now more likely to come from Asia than from Mexico or Latin America. And compared with Americans overall, immigrants today are disproportionately well-educated and entrepreneurial. They are transforming the nation in ways largely ignored by the political jousting over how immigration is affecting America's culture, economy and national security.

As of three years ago, Census figures show, India and China eclipsed Mexico as the top sources of U.S. immigrants, whether authorized or not. In 2013, 147,000 Chinese immigrants and 129,000 Indians came to the U.S., compared with 125,000 Mexicans. Most of the Asian immigrants arrived in the United States legally—through work, student or family visas.

Immigrants are also more likely now to be U.S. citizens. Nearly half of immigrants over the age of 25—18 million people—are naturalized citizens, compared with just 30 percent back in 2000, according to Census figures.

Simultaneously, more Mexicans without documentation are returning home. The number of Mexicans in the United States illegally tumbled nearly 8 percent in the past six years to 5.85 million, the Pew Research Center found. Border Patrol apprehensions, one gauge of illegal crossings, last year reached their lowest point since 1971.

With the share of U.S. residents born abroad at its highest level in a century, immigrants increasingly defy the stereotypes that tend to shape conversations on the issue. Consider:

— About 40 percent of Indian immigrants hold a graduate degree. Fewer than 12 percent of native-born Americans do. And earnings for a median Indian immigrant household exceed $100,000—more than twice the U.S. median.

— A majority of Chinese immigrants have come to the United States to seek education. China has become the dominant source of foreigners attending U.S. universities, with 304,000 student visas in the past academic year. India is second, with 133,000 visas. In addition, a quarter of immigrants from China hold graduate degrees.

— Since 2011, a majority of Indian and Chinese immigrants have been between ages 15 and 29. Their youth means they're likely to have children born as U.S. citizens, who will then become prime contributors to American population growth in the years ahead, according to an analysis by Census officials.

The influx of Asians has not only reshaped the face of America's immigrant population. It has also sharpened the divide within the immigrant population—between well-educated Asians and arrivals from Mexico and Latin America who have little money or education. The result is that America's 40 million-plus immigrants more and more reflect the extremes of America's economic spectrum, from super-rich tech titans to poor agriculture workers.

Yet economists say immigrants from both ends of the divide are benefiting the economy. At a time when the growth of the U.S. workforce has slowed, immigrants and their collective spending have become a key source of economic fuel.

These disparate groups of immigrants have helped reshape towns and cities, populated new suburban housing developments and revived main streets in some decaying rural communities. The changes flash into view on a visit to the political swing state of North Carolina. The proportion of immigrants in the state's population has quadrupled from 1990 to nearly 8 percent. Similar trends have emerged in Georgia, Colorado, Oregon and Washington.

None of these states approaches the more than 20 percent share in California and New York. Yet the transformations are evident in a drive across the dense highways that connect North Carolina's Research Triangle. The suburbs sandwiched among Chapel Hill, Durham and Raleigh have exploded with plazas crowded with upscale lunch spots and designer gyms.

Indian immigrants have put their distinctive stamp on this area. Their prevalence here is similar to the many educated Chinese immigrants who have settled around Los Angeles, San Francisco and New York.

On evenings in the Research Triangle, many of the cars on Aviation Parkway pull off to stop at the 20-acre Hindu Society of North Carolina in Morrisville, which hosts yoga classes and religious services.

In 2000, when the society's temple was built, Morrisville was home to just 230 Indians. Now, there are 4,300. Those with roots in the community dating to the 1960s recall a period when a grocery run for authentic Indian ingredients required a five-hour drive to Washington, D.C. Those treks are no longer necessary.

Their rising numbers have established a broad community of Indians that has made it easier for new arrivals to integrate than it was for prior generations.

"Now, you come from India, you don't really have to know anything else," said Pranav Patel, a 57-year-old software developer. "The system is here to help you adjust. There are no real hardships."

Asked how they have been received in the community, about a dozen Asian immigrants said they have generally been warmly accepted despite the national furor over immigration. One, oncologist, Dr. Neeraj Agrawal, said he could recall a patient having to overcome an initial reluctance to be treated by a foreigner. But that was a rare exception.

"There's a dramatic change in attitudes about skilled, educated immigrants: 'You're welcome. You're a good neighbor. You're a good addition to society,'" said Agrawal, who was born and educated in India.

In August, Gopala went to the Hindu Society to celebrate India's independence day. Over the entrance of the temple is the symbol for "om," representing knowledge—a reminder of education's vaunted status. Music blared over the crowd amid dancing and honors paid to statues of deities. Gopala enjoyed the festivities. Yet she saw few white and black guests sharing in the moment.

Manasi Gopala, a software developer in North Carolina's Research Triangle, works from home in Cary, NC, September 16, 2016. (AP Photo/Gerry Broome)

Weeks later, she wondered: Did part of integrating mean inviting others to share your culture, to welcome neighbors with samosas and other delicacies?

One prominent outsider did show up: Gov. Pat McCrory, a Republican in a heated re-election campaign that has been fueled in part by a crack-down on illegal immigration.

McCrory flattered the crowd.

"This is the best of America," he said, sharing the stage with a life-sized statue of Mahatma Gandhi. "This is the best of India. We work together. We learn together. We can pray together. We love family values together."

Not all immigrant groups enjoy that same Southern hospitality from North Carolina's government.

McCrory has backed laws to deny basic services and forms of identification to immigrants without legal status and their children. The governor signed a law last year barring North Carolina cities from helping unauthorized immigrants, whom he has associated with crime, and overcrowded schools and hospital emergency rooms.

His policies are premised on the belief that less-educated immigrants without legal status are burdens for taxpayers. But the arrival of Mexican immigrants helped save Duplin County, a quiet stretch of leafy tobacco fields and prefab homes about 70 miles south of Raleigh.

Until the 1990s, Duplin County's population had been roughly a flat 40,000 for 50 years. Then Hispanic farmworkers began immigrating, and the population nears 60,000 today. About 7,200 immigrants now live in Duplin County, most from Latin America; there are no clear estimates of how many are there legally.

Nearly three out of four didn't finish high school, but even these immigrants have helped rural North Carolina—opening businesses and keeping farms in operation despite harsh work conditions.

One Mexican immigrant arrived in North Carolina nearly two decades ago illegally, after a brutal crossing where he saw a fellow Mexican robbed. Having dropped out of school at 13 with little fluency in English, he took whatever jobs were available.

Planting and cutting tobacco was the hardest, he said. In one case, a building contractor offered to pay $500 a week, only to give him just $350 after five long days of labor. The immigrant said there was no one to protect him from this abuse.

Ultimately, this immigrant, who agreed to speak only anonymously because of his legal status, saved enough to open a small business.

"For me, this my pueblo," he said of his adopted country. "I love this place."

Americans' sentiments about him and other immigrants have largely hardened along racial, political and demographic lines. Overall feelings toward immigrant workers remain negative. But sentiment has improved since 2006, possibly a sign that the growth of educated immigrants has begun to reshape attitudes, according to a Pew survey released this month.

Two-thirds of Republicans and 54 percent of whites said they think immigration harms U.S. workers. But a majority of Democrats, Hispanics and the college-educated said they felt immigrants made society better off.

By comparison, almost all economists view immigrants as helpful— even essential—for the nation's continued prosperity. On the one hand, some visa programs have deprived U.S. workers of jobs. And some companies have been accused of hiring cheaper foreign workers to replace older workers in similar jobs. But academic research has debunked the claims that immigration on the whole takes jobs away from natives, said Bill Kerr, a professor at Harvard University's Business School whose research has shown that immigration helps business formation.

"Ultimately, our economies are able to grow, absorb people and do a number of dynamic things," Kerr said.

Because of the aging U.S. population causing more retirements, most economists say immigrants are needed to ensure that the workforce increases at a sufficient pace to sustain overall growth in the long term.

Anti-immigration groups such as the Federation for American Immigration Reform argue that the United States should cap all immigration levels. These groups contend that lesser-educated workers from Latin America diminish economic growth because they receive government-funded health care and education. And they argue that the jobs that are going to educated immigrants should be directed toward U.S. citizens.

"Trying to grow your economy through the importation of bodies is rudimentary and Neanderthal-like," said Dan Stein, FAIR's executive director. "It's backward."

Other research disputes this claim, finding value among the largely Hispanic group of less-educated immigrants. For every dollar spent on health care and education, North Carolina got $11 back from Hispanic residents in terms of consumer spending and taxes paid—a finding that includes unauthorized immigrants, said James Johnson, a demographer at the University of North Carolina, Chapel Hill.

While much of the debate has focused on the economic effects of immigration, many opponents fear a burden on taxpayers and the cultural changes in a nation coming to grips with its widening diversity.

The anti-immigrant rhetoric has concerned Gopala. She feels fortunate to no longer be among the millions of foreigners still applying for U.S. residency.

"I got very lucky that my green card was processed when immigration wasn't a bad word," Gopala said.

"America had given me the opportunity to pursue my own life. On the day you're born in India, your life is written. But here, that is not true."

Dallas
Seeing options shrinking, white men ask why

There is an angst and ardor that I've seen repeated in recent years. It seemed to bubble up in opposition to Barack Obama's presidential candidacy, where shouts of "terrorist" and "kill him" could be heard at campaign rallies. That fiery, sometimes unhinged passion, grew in tea party events and, later, in town hall meetings on the Affordable Care Act.

It wasn't limited to a single demographic, of course, but it become clear early on that these feelings had particular resonance among white men. When I spoke about it with Michael Kimmel, who has studied this rage and authored a 2013 book entitled "Angry White Men," he said he never mentioned Donald Trump's name once in his 300-plus-page study.

In retrospect, though, he says Trump was precisely the leader these men were waiting for.

Even five years ago, you saw prescient glimpses of it. Trump had been floating the idea of running for president and was headlining a raucous tea party event that I covered in Florida. He promised if he won the White House, the country would be respected again. His confidence easily convinced the audience, which responded with chants of "Ron, Donald, Run!" and waved signs with his name.

They have become his bedrock support, and while the health care law is etched in history and tea party rallies have faded, that same vocal opposition that I saw beginning eight years ago has found a home in Trump's candidacy. They passionately defend him and find kinship with so many others in their neighborhoods, online, and in a web of conservative radio shows across this country.

I wanted to try and capture the feelings of white men through one of those shows, and was taken by the strength and eloquence of Rick Roberts in Dallas. In my visit to WBAL, I spent a day in the show's control room, where a producer screened callers, and another on the other side of a pane of glass, where halo of red light above Roberts' microphone made known he was on air. And as I followed up with the men who found a home in the show and turned to it to hear their views validated, I heard familiar refrains.

It would be easy to dismiss them with words like racist and sexist and out of touch. They admit they aren't politically correct, but plod on, speaking of jobs disappearing and debt ballooning and morals fading. They use varying words and inflections, but carry a similar message of loss and confusion, of what happened to the country they knew and how they fit into the one they inhabit today.

— Matt Sedensky, AP National Writer

* * *

The voices cascade into the studio, denouncing political hypocrisy and media bias and disappearing values. Hillary Clinton is a liar and a crook, they say; Donald Trump is presidential and successful. By the time the 16th caller reaches the air, Rick Roberts' show has reached an impassioned crescendo of anger and lamentation.

What has happened to this once-great land? What has happened to the better lives our children were promised?

What has happened?

Roberts, WBAP's bearded, rodeo-roping, husky-voiced host, has heard enough.

"I want my country back," he begins.

He repeats that sentence a half-dozen times in a 4½-minute rant that darts from fear of crime to outsourced jobs to political correctness. He pans soulless politicians and has-been celebrities and psycho-babble hug-a-tree experts; he pines for a time when everyone spoke English and looked you in the eye and meant what they said. It's a fervent soliloquy that dismisses transgender people and calls for faith to regain public footing and for economic opportunity to return.

"I want America to be America," he says. "I want some semblance of what this country used to be. It's worth protecting. It's worth defending. I don't recognize this country anymore."

This is a white male voice preaching to a largely white male audience that has expressed many of the same sentiments, in dribs and drabs, in hushed watercooler conversations and boisterous barroom exchanges, around kitchen tables — and most of all, in the course of a presidential campaign in which Trump has become their champion and their hope.

Certainly, not all white males agree. But at this moment in American history, to be white and male means, for many, to question what happened to the opportunities once theirs for the taking, to see others getting ahead and wonder why, to feel centuries of privilege and values slipping away.

"They're taking everything from us," says one of the day's callers, Stephen Sanders. "I don't want my community changed."

The callers express resentment of immigrants who came here illegally, suspicion of Muslims, disdain for gays. They rail against a coarsening of culture, while backing a man who brags about making unwanted sexual advances. They voice bitterness toward a society they see as rallying to save an endangered animal or to lobby for the bathroom rights of transgender children, while seeming to ignore their own pain.

To many, the notion of white men being marginalized is ludicrous, their history a study in power and privilege, from the Founding Fathers to the "Mad Men" era and through their continued dominance in boardrooms and government. Yet they have suffered some real losses, even as they maintain advantages:

— Whites saw their household net worth fall from a median of $192,500 before the Great Recession to $141,900 in 2013, according to a Pew Research Center analysis. (The declines of blacks and Hispanics were far larger, and whites still have an average net worth about 13 times greater than blacks and 10 times greater than Hispanics.)
— Factoring in inflation, white men's salaries have barely budged in the past decade, according to Bureau of Labor Statistics data. (Still, they cash paychecks, on average, far larger than those of women, blacks and Hispanics, and have a lower rate of unemployment.)
— The home ownership rate for whites, 71.5 percent in the second quarter of this year, is down from the same period a decade earlier, according to the U.S. Census Bureau. (Black and Hispanic home-ownership, already lower, dropped at a far sharper rate.)
— White women have overtaken men in earning college degrees, according to census data. (White men still hold a big educational advantage over blacks and Hispanics.)
— The number of incarcerated white men has ballooned, according to the Bureau of Justice Statistics. (Black and Hispanic men remain far more likely to be jailed.)
— Fueled by suicides, drug overdoses and alcohol-related illnesses, mortality rates for middle-age whites have increased even as they continue to fall among middle-age blacks and Hispanics, a shift recorded in a landmark study last year in the Proceedings of the National Academy of Sciences. (Still, white men continue to have a longer life expectancy than black men, according to Centers for Disease Control data, though shorter than Hispanics.)

These are among the changes that have sent white men to Tea Party gatherings, to fractious town hall meetings and, more recently, to Trump's rallies. Some argue, though, that their rage has been misplaced.

"What's made their lives more difficult is not what they think," said Michael Kimmel, a Stony Brook University professor who studies masculinity and wrote the book "Angry White Men." "LGBT people didn't

Radio talk show host Rick Roberts speaks will a caller during his program in Dallas, September 6, 2016. (AP Photo/LM Otero)

outsource their jobs. Minorities didn't cause climate change. Immigrants didn't issue predatory loans from which they now have lost their houses and everything they ever had. These guys are right to be angry, but they're delivering the mail to the wrong address."

The clock hits 2 p.m., and the top-of-the-hour headlines at WBAP advise of a hurricane swirling in the Pacific and a new poll on the Trump-Clinton race. Roberts' show begins every day with the sounds of the country duo Big & Rich.

"I ain't gonna shut my mouth," they sing. "Don't mind if I stand out in a crowd. Just wanna live out loud. Well I know there's got to be a few hundred million more like me."

The host is authoritative but genial. He doesn't yell, hears out the occasional liberal who dials in, sometimes corrects a caller's inaccuracies. He hands a huge swath of his airtime over to listeners.

Fifteen minutes into the broadcast, Roberts reminds his audience he's a registered independent, not a Republican, though he can't recall the last time he gave a Democrat his vote.

"Let's go to Bill in Garland," Roberts says.

The caller dismisses Hillary and Bill Clinton as "liars, cheats and thieves" and says he doesn't think he could vote for the Democrat even if his three grandchildren were held hostage.

181

Reached by phone three days later, he conceded to a reporter that he used an alias. His name is Jim Drahman and he's a 70-year-old computer technician.

"People are afraid to say anything in public," he says, for fear of offending. "They've got to worry about everything they say."

He just wants to be able to go to work and live freely, he says. He doesn't want the government telling him what he can drink or smoke or drive. He knows taxes are a necessity, but believes they should be lower. He views things through his grandchildren's eyes, and worries about terrorism and the economy, but most of all, about the U.S. maintaining its status in the world.

"I just want them to have a country that I can be proud of," he says.

Calls come in at a steady clip, and when Stephen Sanders dials in, he's enraged by a poll showing Clinton making gains in Texas. "Sir, stop yelling," the show's producer says, before typing in a summary of Sanders' tirade for the host: "Allowing illegals to vote is treason."

Sanders is no calmer a day later. He rages against illegal immigration. The media and most politicians have been co-opted into accepting open borders, he says. Those who came here illegally are "continuing to suck on the labors of people who are contributing."

Sanders' father worked in a warehouse but was able to give his family a life of abundance. Jobs were everywhere. You didn't need a college degree or the resulting load of debt. He misses the simplicity of those times, and laments today's pervasive sex, the tattoos and body piercings and bright blue hair. He is 49 and was once an X-ray technician. He says his skill and years of seniority were ignored when he applied for a supervisory job that ultimately went to a black candidate he said "walked right off the street." He later fell into depression and now receives a disability check.

"You're white, you're male, you're the least considered," he says. "As far as white privilege, I see it. I would think it was there if I went to Princeton or Yale or if my name was Hillary or Clinton. As far as me, no."

Despite Trump's privileged upbringing and Ivy League education, Sanders was pleased when the billionaire announced his candidacy; he was thrilled to hear someone give voice to his feelings about immigration and outsourcing and restoring opportunity for guys like him. It felt, he said, like seeing decades of painful history starting to be reversed. He wants to

A supporter of Donald Trump holds a sign reading "Trump has my vote" during a campaign rally attended mostly by whites in Winston-Salem, NC, , July 25, 2016. (AP Photo/Evan Vucci)

return to work. He wants to be productive. He wants to live a better life than his father, but he doesn't.

"The theme about the American experience is to get better and to do more," he says. "I've never experienced it. I've always struggled."

Roberts' show breaks for the news again (a highway accident, a missing man with dementia, more hot weather). He plays a clip of Trump insisting he'll build a border wall and returns to the air calling Clinton "the Teflon mom" before going to a caller—"Jon in Cedar Hill"—who says the former secretary of state should be convicted.

Jon Hayes is deep into his daily radio routine, a listening marathon that starts with the midnight-to-5-a.m. "Red Eye Radio" and ends with Roberts' show, which wraps up at 5 p.m. For Hayes, sleep comes in spurts, including an extended nap during Rush Limbaugh's time slot.

He wonders where the tear-down-this-wall strength of the Reagan era went. He sees modern-day America as an internet-governed, me-me-me culture. Tired of political correctness, he sometimes wears a T-shirt that says, "Prepare To Be Offended."

Hayes once had his own construction business, but he said it folded and he lost his house when it became impossible to compete against the cheap labor of immigrants who came to the U.S. illegally. He fell back on his knowledge of auto mechanics. Though he is 55, he had hoped to retire this year; he has put it off. A grown son still lives at home, and for all the setbacks Hayes has had in his life, he believes he's still able to say something that he's not sure the 29-year-old will: He achieved a better life than his parents.

"I just don't think the opportunity is out there now that there used to be," he says.

He's far from alone in his pessimism. A Kaiser Family Foundation-CNN poll released in September compared white college graduates and the white, black and Hispanic working class. Working-class whites were least likely to say that they're satisfied with their influence in the political process, that the federal government represents their views, and that they believe their children will achieve a better standard of living than themselves. They were most likely to say it has become harder to get ahead financially and find good jobs in recent years, and most likely to blame economic problems on the federal government and immigrants working here illegally.

WBAP estimates Roberts' audience is about two-thirds male and overwhelmingly white, though women and minorities also call in on this day and you needn't look far, even in Roberts' own studio, to find a white man who doesn't subscribe to conservative orthodoxy.

On the other side of the glass from the host, monitoring a bank of four screens and a large audio board, is Randy Williams. Roberts says he's a "hair-on-fire liberal," but the 65-year-old Navy veteran calls himself a fiscal conservative and a social progressive, but mostly a disaffected American.

"Nobody represents my interests," he says. "There's the 5 percent on the far left and the 5 percent on the far right and 90 percent of us are stuck in the middle."

"Ken in Dallas. Ken, I appreciate your patience."

Ken from Dallas is Ken Hindman, a 57-year-old gas tanker driver. He tells Roberts that Clinton is like mobster John Gotti.

Later, he takes a break from driving his 18-wheeler toward Dallas Love Field, pulling over to a rest stop to expand on his views.

He says he doesn't "feel one iota of responsibility" for the wrongs committed against black Americans. When filling out a form asking his race,

Truck driver Ken Hindman, a caller on Rick Roberts radio talk show, says he doesn't "feel one iota of responsibility" for the wrongs committed against black Americans. When he opposed Obama, he complains, he was branded a racist. (AP Photo/LM Otero)

he checks "other." He's tired of labels; when he opposed Obama, he complains, he was branded a racist. Trump, he admits, was not his first choice. But he has earned Hindman's fervent support.

"He says the things that a lot of people that I know feel," he says.

There was a time when white men were the ones earning the paychecks and deciding who pulls the levers of power. Now, many of them say they're just looking to be heard. So when they amass in arenas to hear Trump, or call into Roberts' studio to share their thoughts, their voices carry more than anger. Here, they say, is a wisp of the respect and validation they long to regain.

Roberts sees his "I want my country back" monologue as a tonic for that despair. When you're on the air three hours a day, five days a week, the listener angst can be overwhelming. It was about two years ago when he delivered the rant, impromptu, on a day when he reached a saturation point.

He feels that same anguish. Roberts says his parents were never in his life. He was raised by grandparents and, when they grew too old, he was emancipated at age 15 and landed at a boys' ranch. "I fell on my ass more than I can count," the 53-year-old says, dismissing any thought of privilege he may have inherited. "I didn't feel real privileged at the time."

He scraped his way up, earned an MBA and law degree, and made a career negotiating offshore oil contracts. He started in radio 22 years ago and now presides over a kingdom of white man's woe, listening to talk of disappearing jobs and ballooning debt and fading morals.

He can't remember precisely what prompted his unscripted oratory—maybe what Roberts calls Barack Obama's "apology tour," or perceived pushback against American exceptionalism. It resonated, though, and he keeps an MP3 of the audio on his computer and airs it every now and again.

He clicks the file and it begins to play: "I want my country back, and the only way, the only way I'm ever going to be able to get this country back is if I reach out to the brothers and sisters that all feel the very same way and say, 'Hell, no, you can't have the country.'"

"Stop it! How many different ways do we say stop it!?"

Conclusion
Yearning for unity, enduring divisiveness

Though they live about 1,730 miles apart, though they've never met, though they are of different races and backgrounds, Lauren Boebert and Dorothy Johnson-Speight speak almost in unison when they lament the fracturing of America.

Americans must "come together, be non-judgmental about people and their opinions," says Johnson-Speight. Americans must "come together as one," says Boebert.

And yet these two women stand squarely at the epicenter of American acrimony—territory explored by The Associated Press in "Divided America," a series of stories that surveyed a United States that is far from united.

Boebert owns the gun-friendly Shooters Grill in the aptly named town of Rifle, Colorado, and wears a handgun. Johnson-Speight fights for gun control laws after the 2001 murder of her 24-year-old son Khaaliq Jabbar Johnson, shot seven times in a dispute over a Philadelphia parking spot.

Their differences are stark, but their yearning for a more civil and less divided nation is genuine. In that, they mirror other Americans interviewed over the past six months. They are caught up in a campaign that magnified its disagreements, and left them longing for harmony; they live in a country that cannot square its present with its pedigree as "one nation, under God, indivisible."

The fact is, America's differences are real, and cannot be glossed over.

In Missoula, Montana, an effort to welcome dozens of refugees—Congolese, Afghans, Syrians—was met with demonstrations and angry confrontations. "I didn't do this to be controversial. I didn't do this to stir the pot," says Mary Poole, one of the leaders of the refugee project—but she did. Two patriotic visions came into conflict: the America that welcomes the huddled masses yearning to breathe free, and the America still shaken by terrorist attacks of Sept. 11, 2001, and in the years since, insisting on homeland security above all.

On New York's Staten Island, police and the policed struggle to coexist. On an island that is home to 3,000 police officers, a black man suspected of selling loose cigarettes died in an encounter with police in 2014. The black community knows the police do an important job, but it is deeply distrustful after the death of Eric Garner and other violent encounters with authority. Police, meanwhile, feel unappreciated, their character impugned. "I think the divide is worse than it should be and more than people think it is," says retired detective Joe Brandefine.

At the Christian Fellowship Church in Benton, Kentucky, pastor Richie Clendenen tells his congregation, "There's nobody more hated in this nation than Christians." Evangelical Christians' numbers are in decline, their political clout diminished. On signal issues—particularly same-sex marriage—they have lost, at least for the moment. They are angry and frustrated and unwilling to surrender. "We are moving more and more in conflict with the culture and with other agendas," says David Parish, a former pastor at Christian Fellowship.

There's so much more: Americans split on climate change, between those who say it is an existential threat and those who deny it is happening or at least that man has anything to do with it. Even as they contemplate electing the first woman president, even as women take on combat roles, Americans are struggling with a misogynistic backlash, online and in real life. Then there's the gun debate, which Adam Winkler, a constitutional law professor at UCLA says is "more polarized and sour than any time before in American history."

There is common ground. At the Annin Flagmakers factory in South Boston, Virginia, seamstress Emily Bouldin says Americans "may be divided on some things, but when it comes down to the most important things we come together." Nearly all Americans, according to surveys, believe in small business, the public schools, helping the less fortunate and caring for veterans.

Some differences, though, are profound and lasting, having less to do with what people think and more to do with where they fall—on which side of the line between prosperity and ill-fortune.

In Logan, West Virginia, in central Appalachia, the decline of the coal industry has brought a population drain, rampant drug abuse, heightened poverty (cremations are up because folks can't afford caskets) and deep resentment that fed support for Republican Donald Trump: "I don't know what's in his head, what his vision is for us," said Ashley Kominar, a mother of three whose husband lost his job in the mines. "But I know he has one and that's what counts."

The recovery from the Great Recession has left behind a lot of rural America. The Washington-based Economic Innovation Group found that half of the new business growth over the past four years was concentrated in just 20 populous counties, and three quarters of the nation's economically distressed ZIP codes are in rural areas.

The recovery meant little to workers in Hannibal, Ohio, where Chinese competition resulted in the loss of the largest employer, the Ormet aluminum plant.

And it meant little to students in Waukegan, Illinois; poor school districts had no way to make up funding losses when federal stimulus money dried up. So while the nearby Stevenson district spends close to $18,800 per student, Waukegan spends about $12,600. Its students must cope with a high school that is often badly maintained, where as many as 28 students share a single computer.

That Stevenson is mostly white and Waukegan is mostly minority should come as little surprise. The racial divide endures, at least in some part because minorities continue to be significantly underrepresented in Congress and nearly every state legislature, an AP analysis found. Thanks to gerrymandering and voting patterns, non-Hispanic whites make up a little over 60 percent of the U.S. population, but still hold more than 80 percent of all congressional and state legislative seats.

An example: African-Americans represent more than a fifth of Delaware residents, but for the past 22 years Margaret Rose Henry has been the state's only black senator.

"If there were more black elected officials, we would have a better chance to get something done," Henry says.

Much of this is not new. As much as Americans like to recall the past as a rosy Norman Rockwell illustration, they have been at odds from the start—thousands of British loyalists battled their revolutionary neighbors in the colonies, North and South went to war over race, labor and management fought for decades, often violently, and the Vietnam era was awash with vitriol.

If today's divisiveness is different, some say, perhaps it is because of a lack of leadership.

"Yes, America is great. It could be a lot be a lot better if the politicians weren't fighting each other all the time," says Rodney Kimball, a stove dealer in West Bethel, Maine.

Elvin Lai, a San Diego hotelier, says the voters themselves must accept much of the blame.

"I do believe that our political system is broken," he says. "I do believe that a person that is centered and is really there to bring the country together won't get the votes because they're not able to speak to the passionate voters who want to see change."

It's those passionate voters, after all, who cocoon themselves with the likeminded, watching Fox News if they lean right or reading Talking Points Memo if they're on the left. In their ideological segregation, their minds are not open to compromise.

Take gun control. For all the nastiness surrounding the issue, a Pew Research Center poll in August showed 85 percent of American supported background checks for purchases at gun shows and in private sales, 79 percent support laws to prevent the mentally ill from buying guns, 70 percent approve of a federal database to track gun sales.

Dorothy Johnson-Speight, who founded the anti-violence, anti-gun group Mothers in Charge after her son's death, says these are steps well worth taking. "We don't want to take the rights of responsible gun owners away," she says.

Her aim is peace—both in the streets and in the public sphere.

"We've got to find a way to be more accepting of one another, more tolerant of each other," she says. "We have more things in common that we do that are different and we need to find those commonalities in order to live in peace."

Lauren Boebert calls most gun measures "crazy," but she is not skeptical about the ability of the American people to rise above division, on this and other issues.

"Right now, we're using our rights to tear each other apart," she says, passionately. "Freedom of speech, it's just being used to say whatever mean, harmful, violent thing you can. . . . That's not what it's for. You also have the freedom to lift them up and to hold them up and edify them. Let's come together, let's unify as Americans, all of us."

— by Jerry Schwartz, Deputy Director of Top Stories/Enterprise

Appendix

Photo Gallery
Images of Americans' daily lives

The idea of the Divided America Moments photo project was to explore the concept of a single place, a moment in the day of Americans that defines them, their beliefs, and the issue that is most important to them. We wanted to take the reader away from the rallies and campaign events and into the lives of ordinary Americans who are directly impacted by some of the most divisive issues this election year.

The goal was to focus on a single, intimate storytelling image that could provide insight into a person's life and why they feel the way they do about their particular issue. We hoped to visualize these personal moments for the reader.

A team of about a dozen photographers across the country researched immigration, the economy, the environment, gun rights, social values like abortion, gay rights and conservative christian beliefs, and race to find the right characters of different viewpoints whose lives are impacted by these issues then provide a strong visual story. We wanted to photograph these moments in a personal way to allow the reader to relate to someone they've never met and in some cases even disagree with.

The challenges we faced in trying to do this felt like 'finding a needle in a haystack'. First we had to find people who could point to a moment in their daily life that was directly affected by these issues. Then, in addition to being articulate in an interactive interview, we had to make sure that the moment was a visual one. Someone having to file additional paperwork for their taxes because of economic policies just wouldn't translate into an intimate moment. Not all issues or situations were photogenic but we felt they were part of the divineness so regardless, we tried to push the access to make it as intimate as possible. We really had to gain the trust of subjects to let us into their personal space, either at home or work or wherever the issue came into play.

In the end, 26 characters, from age 17 to 73, from California to Maine were represented in a photo gallery of these singular moments as well as an interactive feature with a video portrait, additional photos and audio interviews. We hope with this project by letting ordinary Americans on both sides of a contentious issue tell their stories, perhaps, if only for a few seconds, we can offer a little understanding on the divisiveness of these issues.

— David Goldman, AP Photographer

* * *

A woman sleeps in her car, waiting to receive free dental care at a clinic in rural Virginia. Another peers though a fence at the Mexican border to see the grandmother she left behind 18 years before, when she was brought to the United States as a toddler.

Health care and immigration are two of the most contentious issues of this most contentious election year, but they are not merely grist for politics and politicians. Americans like these women, Lesia Crigger and Eva Lara, are dealing with them in nearly every moment of their everyday lives.

A team of Associated Press photographers traversed the country to record those moments. Each set out to capture intimate images to illustrate the human side of immigration, the economy, the environment, gun rights, social values like abortion, gay rights and conservative Christian beliefs, and race.

The result: A mosaic of a people at a singular time, struggling to extend the American project through the treacherous shoals of the 21st century.

Tim Foley checks a map during a surveillance patrol in Sasabe, AZ, May 11, 2016. Foley, a former construction foreman founded Arizona Border Recon, a group of armed volunteers who dedicate themselves to border surveillance. (AP Photo/Gregory Bull)

Eva Lara and her brother, Bryan, talk through a border fence in San Diego to their grandmother, Juana Lara, who stands on the Mexican side on May 1, 2016 . It was the first time Eva had seen her grandmother since she left Mexico at the age of 3 with her parents. Eva lives in the United States legally through legislation that temporarily prevents young immigrants from being deported. She went to see her grandmother through the fence on her 21st birthday. "This was probably the best birthday gift I could get, you know, just seeing her. It was very emotional," she said. "It was too much to take in, very overwhelming." (AP Photo/Gregory Bull)

Duncan Wallace plays golf in Vista, CA, on May 4, 2016. Wallace, who owns a medical supplies company, said he's been a conservative for 50 years, ever since he read Barry Goldwater's book, "Conscience of a Conservative." (AP Photo/Gregory Bull)

Business owner Duncan Wallace displays a picture of himself and his wife standing alongside former Republican presidential candidate Ben Carson. "I think we punish success, actually," he said. "I know a lot of people who are quite successful, and they are paying an awful lot of money in taxes. They are paying for people who don't have their oar in the water." (AP Photo/Gregory Bull)

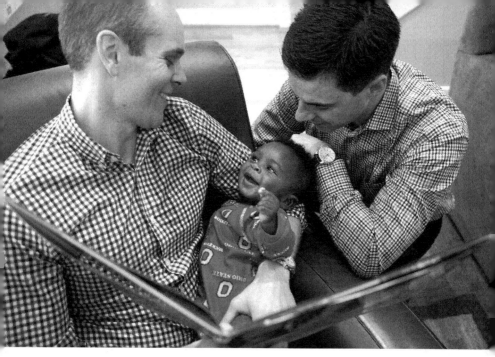

On May 19, 2016, Gregg Pitts, left, and Brooks Brunson read to their son, Thomas Brunson-Pitts, 6 months, before heading to work in the morning at their home in Washington. Married in 2013, Brooks Brunson and Gregg Pitts always knew they wanted to have a family together, and were delighted when they were able to start the adoption process for their son shortly after beginning to look for a match in 2015. The child's birth mother had no problem with a same-sex couple adopting the baby. The District of Columbia legalized gay marriage in 2010. (AP Photo/Jacquelyn Martin)

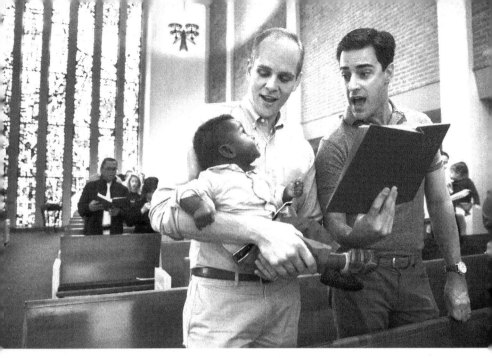

Gregg Pitts holds their son Thomas Brunson-Pitts, 6 months, as his husband Brooks Brunson, sings to the baby as the family attends church at Capitol Hill United Methodist Church in Washington, May 8, 2016. "We're an interracial same-sex couple family," says Brunson, "But our day-to-day life is picking up dry cleaning, getting to work on time, making sure Thomas has his bottle prepared - we're the most boring people I know. But then when I take a step back I realize we are very unique. But I believe this is exactly where God wants me to be." (AP Photo/Jacquelyn Martin)

Hundreds of people line up in the early morning to attend the Remote Area Medical (RAM) clinic in Smyth County, VA., April 29, 2016. RAM provides free medical care to people who do not have health insurance in several states across the country. Specializing in free dental, vision, and medical care in isolated and poverty stricken communities, the group sets up mobile medical centers and is having their 800th such event this year. "I've done foreign volunteer missions before," says volunteer dentist Mark Copas, "but never domestic. These cases are just as bad as what I've seen in third world countries." (AP Photo/Jacquelyn Martin)

Lesia Crigger, 47, of Woodlawn, VA, who is hoping to get fitted for dentures, lights a cigarette as she sits in a car that she slept in overnight with her sister Rhonda Gravley, 52, of Galax, VA., right, as they wait for the Remote Area Medical event to open at dawn in Smyth County, VA. on April 29, 2016. Gravley, who is attending Remote Area Medical for the first time, is there to attend the dental clinic. Neither Gravley nor her sister have dental insurance and cannot afford to pay for it on their own. "I want all of my teeth pulled," says Gravley, "they're all hurting me." Volunteer dentist Mark Copas ended up extracting several of Gravley's teeth. (AP Photo/Jacquelyn Martin)

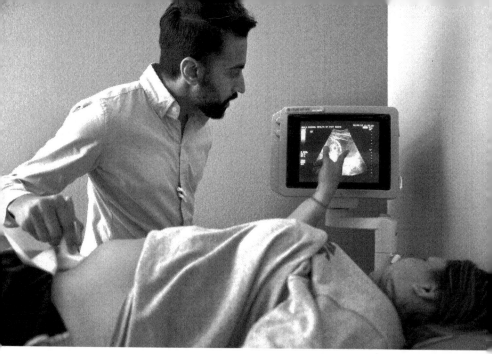

Dr. Bhavik Kumar, 31, listens to a question from a patient seeking an abortion during her ultrasound at the Whole Woman's Health clinic in Fort Worth, TX, June 3, 2016. Women considering abortion are required by the state to have a sonogram that they must be offered the chance to view, although they can refuse to look. There is then a required 24-hour waiting period after the initial consultation. Some must travel long distances twice in order to complete the procedure. This patient, who was 6-weeks pregnant and has a previous child, took the sonogram photograph home with her and scheduled the abortion procedure for the next day. In order to serve the women who depend on a dwindling number of abortion providers in Texas, Kumar commutes across the state to clinics in San Antonio and Fort Worth. "We know the need is there," says Kumar. "I feel morally and ethically obligated to do this work." (AP Photo/ Jacquelyn Martin)

Artemisa Cerda of San Antonio protests abortion outside of Whole Woman's Health in San Antonio on June 2, 2016. Cerda says she protests at the clinic four to five times a week. "I'm here for God because he calls us to love everybody," she says, "born and unborn." She hopes her presence will help change someone's mind about having an abortion. Whole Woman's Health is one of the few abortion providers left in Texas amid strict state legislation on the procedure. (AP Photo/Jacquelyn Martin)

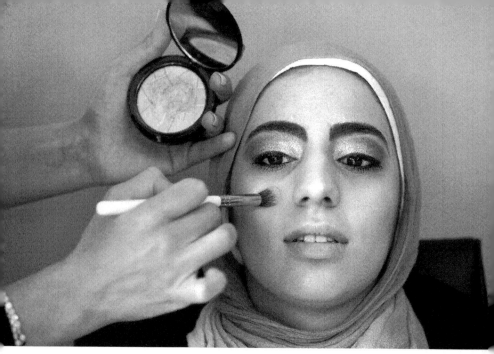

Hannah Shraim, 17, has her makeup done by Farah Kuriashi as she prepares to attend Northwest High School's senior prom. Senior class president and an observant Muslim, Shraim prays five times a day and hopes to become an advocate for Muslims in the United States. After convincing her parents that she was ready for the responsibility of wearing the hijab, she began wearing the Islamic headscarf in the 10th grade. It was a decision her parents were concerned about due to their fears of how strangers might treat her. (AP Photo/Jacquelyn Martin)

Hannah Shraim, right, dances next to Jahnavi Muralidarin during Northwest High School's senior prom held at the Fillmore Theater in Silver Spring, MD, on May 13, 2016. Although not the only Muslim student attending her diverse high school's prom, she was the only student wearing a hijab among the hundreds of sequined dancers that evening. (AP Photo/Jacquelyn Martin)

Karen Fagan, right, participates in an interfaith community event on May 9, 2016 in Pomona, CA. Fagan's ex-husband, Harry Bowman, a father of her two daughters was killed in last year's San Bernardino terrorist attack. She believes that the country should accept Syrian refugees. (AP Photo/Jae C. Hong)

Karen Fagan attends a church service in La Verne, CA. The tragedy of her ex-husband's death during the San Bernardino shootings hasn't changed her belief in acceptance. "America is full of lots of different people from lots of different places," said Fagan. "It saddens me that America is no longer the place where people can come to escape oppression... It's our obligation as Americans and Christians." (AP Photo/Jae C. Hong)

Xiomara Hernandez, 4, pats the shoulder of her father, James, in the lobby area of the Union Rescue Mission on May 8, 2016, in Los Angeles. "Being homeless is very depressing. I feel like I couldn't take care of my family, but also being on Skid Row is very depressing, looking at all these people out here addicted to drugs," said James. (AP Photo/Jae C. Hong)

Homeless Mariah Hernandez, left, zips up the jacket of her 4-year-old daughter Xiomara while playing on the rooftop of the Union Rescue Mission in Los Angeles. Originally from Houston, the family moved to California with their two daughters to try to find a better future for their family. They want to make enough money to rent a small apartment, but at the moment, they're staying at a family shelter on Skid Row. (AP Photo/Jae C. Hong)

Eel grass grows in sediment at Lowell's Cove in Harpswell, Maine, where marine biol-
ogist Diane Cowan has been recording data on juvenile lobsters for the past 24 years.
Cowan says the rise of sea level has ruined some of her sites, including this once rocky
location. (AP Photo/Robert F. Bukaty)

Richard Sawyer, Jr., heads home after a disappointing day of lobstering off Groton, CN on May 2, 2016. Sawyer says lobstering was lucrative for many years but fears those days will never return to Long Island Sound. (AP Photo/Robert F. Bukaty)

Billy Inman, right, and wife Kathy visit the grave of their son on his birthday, May 23, 2016, in Woodstock, GA. A Mexican national in the country illegally crashed his vehicle into one driven by Billy who had stopped for a red light in 2000. The impact killed the Inman's 16-year-old son Dustin and the family dog and left Kathy with serious injuries. In the wake of Dustin's death, the Inmans have become involved in seeking stricter enforcement of laws to combat illegal immigration. (AP Photo/David Goldman)

John Lazzari Jr., 47, jumps over the fence at Naval Outlying Field Silverhill to demonstrate how easy undocumented, unaccompanied children will be able to jump the fence near his home in Daphne, AL. Government officials are deciding whether to put an undocumented, unaccompanied children's camp at the site. Lazzari says that he worries about the safety of his family. "I'm against the refugees coming next to my home because of the unknown, what if they are terrorists or violent youth? Everything I hear about the refugees is bad. I want my family safe." Lazzari says. (AP Photo/Brynn Anderson)

Divided America: An Inside Look

A Q&A with Brian Carovillano, AP Vice President for U.S. News

AP: Can you describe the deliberations among editors and reporters that led to an America divided as the primary story and the decision to tell this story through a long-running series called "Divided America"?

BC: On the one hand, every election year presents an opportunity to get a sense of what people are thinking and experiencing in their communities. But I think it's fair to say that those of us who have been doing this for a long time have never seen an election year quite like this one.

We started talking about this effort early in the year. And from the beginning, it seemed to demand something more comprehensive and ambitious than what we've done in the past. So we sent a lot of really smart journalists out to just talk to people and get a sense of what they were feeling.

What they found out was not exactly what we expected. Yes, there is this sense that we are divided as a nation. But it's not as simple as Republican/Democrat or liberal/conservative. There are so many divisions along so many lines. And that reflects the fabric of who we are as a society. A person's identity is much more than just their race, their political party, their job. It's all of those things, and more. You might think you know how an evangelical Christian from the South is going to vote. But what if that person is also a Hispanic millennial and a union member? People defy easy characterization.

So, all of that led us to the conclusion that we needed much more than a story or even a series of stories and made this a major area of focus for several months, with the goal of attacking it from as many angles as we could.

AP: How did the findings and conclusions of "Divided America" reflect the social currents underlying the mostly unanticipated popularity of presidential candidates Donald Trump and Bernie Sanders?

BC: If there's one thing a broad swath of Americans can agree on, it's that their government is broken. The approval numbers for various institutions are falling off the bottom of the chart.

And that has created an opening for the two outsider candidates with very different messages that ultimately played to the same sense of dissatisfaction in the electorate. The Trump base and the Sanders base may have been at opposite ends of the spectrum, politically, but what they had in common was a sense that the system is not working for them.

Then overlay some pretty harsh economic realities in many parts of the country. We heard this from a lot of people: "The government keeps telling me the economy is all rosy, but I used to have a full-time job, and now I only have part-time work at a lower wage." So we decided to look into that and found there's a lot to that. That a lot of people have had that experience and that the data backs it up.

And finally, Trump's message had particularly resonated with a subset of this group. These folks are mostly white, they have suffered since the recession, they feel the government has failed them, and see the country's changing demographics as part of the reason for it. For better or worse, Trump has animated those feelings in people and they are voting for him.

AP: What have been some of the bigger surprises in the reporting?

BC: One of the biggest surprises had been the degree to which we are united – that is, not divided. Across all these different groups there was widespread agreement that the idea of America, as a place where you can live your life the way you want to live it, is alive and well. The importance of education, of people working together for the greater good—those are common themes we heard from people across the spectrum. Some might feel our best days are behind us; some might think they're still in the future; and some might think we've never been better than we are right now. But those common feelings are out there.

AP: How did AP's member news organizations using this material in their local markets?

BC: We've had seen a lot of member news organizations devoting significant space to the series on both their print and digital platforms. And these stories are pretty evergreen and can be used anytime, so we expect it to have a fairly long tail. What's gratifying is not only that they used our content, but also used the data to show how these divisions and trends are playing out in their own communities.

A Message from Mal Leary

President and Managing Editor of NFOIC

For more than 25 years, the National Freedom of Information Coalition (NFOIC) (www.nfoic.org) has been a national beacon for FOI, access and openness in government and in public institutions at the state and local levels. The national coalition serves as an umbrella of support and action for 42 state and regional affiliates representing 46 states whose members include journalists, attorneys and government watchdog advocates across the country.

Ensuring freedom of information needs champions and a coordinated response. Our objective is to facilitate a national network of first amendment and open government overseers to gain the greatest possible leverage from the expertise our state coalition groups bring to the FOI movement. At a time when the nation's traditional information systems are undergoing massive transformation, it is our job to ensure citizens and journalists are able to maintain control over the instruments they have created.

Each day a resident, journalist, student, and business owner is denied information about a public meeting, document or conversation by their local, state or federal government, or by a public institution such as a school board, utility or university. In this day of advanced information and communication technology, it is inexplicable why these institutions have not created an environment of more openness, transparency and accessibility. Instead, in many cases an opposite reaction has occurred. These public bodies have created new and innovative obstacles to obtain information and to provide access to the interactions of their public officials.

Open record laws, and a determined public and news media to exercise them, have exposed alarming events carried out by public institutions and their agencies. Accessing information about health concerns at water utilities, unprovoked police shootings, illegal dumping of toxic wastes, and public funds used to pay exorbitant fees to private attorneys by government officials to defend FOI violations are just some of the examples.

Freedom of information is largely a local issue, decided and governed at the state, county, or municipal levels. There, protection of the right to access public records is critical. NFOIC reflects a strong team representing a diverse and experienced talent pool with expertise in journalism, media law, public policy and advocacy, and social media.

With a strong and active state affiliate network, NFOIC is the main player in state and local level public record access efforts. NFOIC and its members represent the primary (and arguably, only) systematic, organized effort to address transparency issues at the state and local government levels. This places NFOIC in a unique position to facilitate critical bi-directional communications to identify and address local/state FOI issues or trends for national advocacy and vice versa.

http://nfoic.org/

Please support our efforts by making a donation
http://www.nfoic.org/joincontributedonate

Acknowledgments

The Associated Press would like to thank all those at home and abroad who participated in sharing their concerns, challenges, hopes, dreams and points of view with AP's team of investigative journalists. Additionally, special thanks to Kathleen Carroll, Brian Carovillano, Jerry Schwartz, Sarah Nordgren, Jessica Bruce, Paul Colford, Lauren Easton, Mike Bowser, Nicole Timme, Tommy Browne, Youyou Zhou, Jaime Holguin, Phil Holm, Lisa Gibbs, Pauline Arrillaga, John Daniszewski, Chris Sullivan, Fred Monyak, Jeannie Ohm, Denise Vance, Vaughan Morrison, Matthew Burgoyne, Santiago Lyon, David Goldman, Denis Paquin, Chris Hulme, Marjorie Miller, Kristin Gazlay, Raghu Vadarevu, Anna Johnson, Shelley Acoca, Amanda Barrett, Ted Anthony, Kevin Callahan, Peter Costanzo, and all the dedicated reporters and photographers whose work is featured in this book.

AP Bylines and Contributors

Preface: Pondering whether America's still great
by Jay Reeves and Robin McDowell
Contributors: Mike Householder and Bob Bukaty

Evangelicals feel alienated, anxious
by Rachel Zoll
Contributors: Allen G. Breed and David Goldman

Neighborhoods at Odds over Refugees
by Sharon Cohen

Minorities missing in many legislatures
by David Lieb

Constructing our own intellectual ghettos
by David Bauder

Rosy economic averages bypass many in US
by Christopher S. Rugaber
Contributors: Nicholas Riccardis and Adrian Sainz

Gun views fractious even as fewer bear arms
by Matt Sedensky
Contributors: Larry Fenn and Angeliki Kastanis

Town and country offer differing realities
by Nicholas Riccardi
Contributors: Julie Bykowicz and Angeliki Kastanis,

Bridging the gap between police, policed
by Adam Geller

To some, Trump is a desperate survival bid
by Claire Galofaro
Contributors: Angeliki Kastanis

Clinton highlights lack of women in office
by Christina A. Cassidy

Even in fractured land, there's much unity
by Matt Sedensky
Contributors: David Sterrett
Sidebar: America in one word?
by Matt Sedensky

Arrogant, nice, tech-savvy, free
by Vijay Joshi
Contributors: Charmaine Noronha in Toronto; Jim Gomez in Manila, Philippines; Mauricio Cuevas and Ariel Fernandez in Havana; Jan M. Olsen in Copenhagen, Denmark; Dong Tongjian in Beijing; Thomas Cytrynowicz in New Delhi; Moshe Edri in Jerusalem; Mohammad Aouti in Beirut; Alexander Roslyakov in Moscow; Mari Yamaguchi in Tokyo

Tempers and Temperatures Rise
by Seth Borenstein

Diverse millennials are no voting monolith
by Gillian Flaccus
Contributors: Tamara Lush and Martha Irvine

Will Trump energize the Latino vote?
by Nicholas Riccardi
Contributors: Will Weissert and Russell Contreras and Sergio Bustos

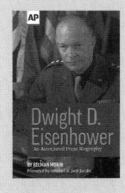

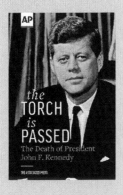